Charged with Grandeur

Charged with Grandeur

A Book of Ignatian Inspiration

edited by

Jim Manney

LOYOLA PRESS.
A JESUIT MINISTRY
Chicago

LOYOLA PRESS.
A JESUIT MINISTRY

3441 N. Ashland Avenue
Chicago, Illinois 60657
(800) 621-1008
www.loyolapress.com

Art credit: Tezzstock, Veer

Library of Congress Cataloging-in-Publication Data
   Charged with grandeur / compiled and edited by Jim Manney.
      p. cm.
   Includes bibliographical references.
   ISBN-13: 978-0-8294-3613-6
   ISBN-10: 0-8294-3613-8
1. Ignatius, of Loyola, Saint, 1491-1556. Exercitia spiritualia.
2. Spirituality--Catholic Church. 3. Spiritual exercises. I. Manney,
Jim.
   BX2179.L8C43 2011
   248.3—dc23

                                                        2011023863

Printed in the United States of America
11 12 13 14 15 16 Bang 10 9 8 7 6 5 4 3 2 1

Contents

Preface

This book takes its title from the first line of a famous poem by the Jesuit Gerard Manley Hopkins: "The world is charged with the grandeur of God." I like "charged." God's grandeur crackles like electricity—powerful, even dangerous. Hopkins continues. God's grandeur "will flame out, like shining from a shook foil." Another image: "it gathers to a greatness, like the ooze of oil." Crackling, gleaming, inexorably growing—what a vivid depiction of the presence of God in our world!

God in the world was Ignatius of Loyola's central preoccupation. He perceived God as active, busy, *here*. This was the God whom the vain and hot-tempered soldier Inigo Loyola met while recovering from battle injuries—a God who spoke to him, bathed him in goodness, called him to a new life, and put him to work. The great work of Ignatius's life was to show others how to meet this God for themselves.

From this work has flowed the great river of Ignatian spirituality. This outlook has become many things in our times. It's a way of praying, a point of view about God, and a practical guide to everyday life. The Ignatian view holds that we can know and love God by joining ourselves to God's work in the world. Its signature idea is that God can be found in all things. "All things" are not God; that's pantheism. Rather, "all things" is where God is to be found—in work and relationships, in cities and suburbia, at the mall and in the home, in business meetings, volunteer projects, factories, classrooms, museums, and theaters. As Gerard Manley Hopkins put it, "To lift up the hands in prayer gives God glory, but a man with a dung fork in his hand, a woman with a slop pail, gives him glory too."

This book consists of selections from writers thinking in the tradition of Ignatius. I hope it demonstrates the range, depth, and relevance of Ignatian spirituality. These writers show how Ignatian insights can breathe new life into relationships and help us make decisions. Some of these selections look at Ignatian traditions of prayer. Some examine Ignatius's emphasis on spiritual freedom and the importance he ascribed to imagination in prayer. Others look at what it means to be a contemplative in action. Many of these selections look at Ignatius himself, and at his great book *The Spiritual Exercises*.

I hope it will help you find God in all things.

Jim Manney

Finding God in All Things

Seeking God's Presence

Ignatius of Loyola

They should practice the seeking of God's presence in all things, in their conversations, their walks, in all that they see, taste, hear, understand, in all their actions, since His Divine Majesty is truly in all things by His presence, power, and essence.

Letters of Saint Ignatius of Loyola

Praying the Examen

Jim Manney

Ignatius of Loyola developed the Examen as a way to find God in all things. It's a time set aside for thankful reflection on where God is in your everyday life. These steps, which most people take more or less in order, usually take 15 to 20 minutes per day.

1. Ask God for light. Begin by asking God for the grace to pray, to see, and to understand.

2. Give thanks. Look at your day in a spirit of gratitude. Everything is a gift from God.

3. Review the day. Guided by the Holy Spirit, look back on your day. Pay attention to your experience. Look for God in it.

4. Look at what's wrong. Face up to failures and shortcomings. Ask forgiveness for your faults. Ask God to show you ways to improve.

5. Look toward the day to come. Where do you need God today? What can you do today?

The Examen looks for signs of God's presence in the events of the day—lunch with a friend, a walk in the park, a kind word from a colleague, a challenge met, a duty discharged. The Examen looks at your conscious experience. The ebb and flow of your moods and feelings are full of spiritual meaning. Nothing is so trivial that it's meaningless.

A Simple, Life-Changing Prayer

Nothing Human Is Merely Human

Ronald Modras

The Ignatian ideal is that now we can recall and relive an experience of "union and familiarity" with God that uplifts and sustains us no matter the distractions of our work or banality of our lives.

Here is the basis for finding God not only in all things but in the flurry of everyday life. Nothing human is merely human. No common labor is merely common. Classrooms, hospitals, and artists' studios are sacred spaces. No secular pursuit of science is merely secular. The hand of the creator can be detected by looking at galaxies through telescopes or examining cellular life in laboratories. Retreatants return to their supposedly dull, humdrum lives with a new vision and appreciation of God's operative presence. Like Ignatius after his experience at the Cardoner River, we see things differently. We get a new sense of what Jesuit poet Gerard Manley Hopkins meant when he wrote, "The world is charged with the grandeur of God."

Ignatian Humanism

There Is Always Something to Pray About

Dennis Hamm, SJ

1. *There is always something to pray about.* For a person who does this kind of prayer at least once a day, there is never the question: What should I talk to God about? Until you die, you always have a past 24 hours, and you always have some feelings about what's next.

2. *The gratitude moment is worthwhile in itself.* "Dedicate yourselves to gratitude," Paul tells the Colossians. Even if we drift off into slumber after reviewing the gifts of the day, we have praised the Lord.

3. *We learn to face the Lord where we are, as we are.* There is no other way to be present to God, of course, but we often fool ourselves into thinking that we have to "put on our best face" before we address our God.

4. *We learn to respect our feelings.* Feelings count. They are morally neutral until we make some choice about acting upon or dealing with them. But if we don't attend to them, we miss what they have to tell us about the quality of our lives.

5. *Praying from feelings, we are liberated from them.* An unattended emotion can dominate and manipulate

us. Attending to and praying from and about the persons and situations that give rise to the emotions help us to cease being unwitting slaves of our emotions.

6. *We actually find something to bring to confession.* That is, we stumble across our sins without making them the primary focus.

7. *We can experience an inner healing.* People have found that praying about (as opposed to fretting about or denying) feelings, leads to a healing of mental life.

"Rummaging for God: Praying Backwards through Your Day"

The World Is Charged with the Grandeur of God

Gerard Manley Hopkins, SJ

The world is charged with the grandeur of God.
It will flame out, like shining from shook foil;
It gathers to a greatness, like the ooze of oil
Crushed. Why do men then now not reck his rod?
Generations have trod, have trod, have trod;
And all is seared with trade; bleared, smeared with toil;
And wears man's smudge and shares man's smell: the soil
Is bare now, nor can foot feel, being shod.

And for all this, nature is never spent;
There lives the dearest freshness deep down things;
And though the last lights off the black West went,
Oh, morning, at the brown brink eastward, springs—
Because the Holy Ghost over the bent
World broods with warm breast and with ah! bright
    wings.

Poems of Gerard Manley Hopkins

Ignatius Found God Everywhere

James Martin, SJ

At the heart of what can seem like frenetic activity was an intimate relationship with God, which Ignatius often found difficult to put into words. His private journals show minuscule notations crowded beside his entries for daily Mass. As scholars have concluded, these indicate, among other things, those times when he wept during Mass, overwhelmed by love for God. Ignatius found God *everywhere*: in the poor, in prayer, in the Mass, in his fellow Jesuits, in his work, and, most touchingly, on a balcony of the Jesuit house in Rome, where he loved to gaze up silently at the stars at night. During these times he would shed tears in wonder and adoration. His emotional response to the presence of God in his life gives the lie to the stereotype of the cold saint.

Ignatius was a mystic who loved God with an intensity rare even for saints. He wasn't a renowned scholar like Augustine or Aquinas, not a martyr like Peter or Paul, not a great writer like Teresa or Benedict, and perhaps not a beloved personality like Francis or Thérèse. But he loved God and loved the world, and those two things he did quite well.

My Life with the Saints

Six Characteristics of Ignatian Spirituality

George W. Traub, SJ

Here is a description of the Ignatian/Jesuit vision.

- It sees life and the whole universe as a gift calling forth wonder and gratefulness.

- It gives ample scope to imagination and emotion as well as intellect.

- It seeks to find the divine in all things—in all peoples and cultures, in all areas of study and learning, in every human experience, and (for the Christian) especially in the person of Jesus.

- It cultivates critical awareness of personal and social evil, but points to God's love as more powerful than any evil.

- It stresses freedom, need for discernment, and responsible action.

- It empowers people to become leaders in service, men and women for others, whole persons of solidarity, building a more just, humane world.

Ignatian Spirituality Reader

Dwelling in Gratitude for What God Has Given

Vinita Hampton Wright

Create a physical space in which you can focus on and enjoy creation. It could be a single potted plant or window box, a bird feeder, a window with a view of the evening or morning sky. Try to involve all your senses as you receive and appreciate what God has given you.

Go through a day—or through a single hour—and discipline yourself to attend to each moment as it comes and to note what is praiseworthy in that moment. Try to build this habit of dwelling completely in the moment at hand rather than in the past or future.

Identify some task you have accomplished and come up with a little celebration of it. This can be private or with friends.

Write a poem about one of your significant relationships. Make it a poem of wonder and praise.

Choose a natural process to enter more intentionally. You might try eating much more slowly and mindfully, thoroughly tasting the food. Or you could notice, over the next few nights, what your process is like for falling asleep. Allow yourself to enjoy the natural tension and release of ordinary processes in your life.

Days of Deepening Friendship

The Whole Panoply of Human Drama

David L. Fleming, SJ

Jesus' way of praying is more important than the words he taught us. We are personally familiar with God ("*our* Father"). We reverence him ("who art in heaven," "hallowed be thy name"). We share God's desires ("thy kingdom come," "thy will be done"). We ask for what we need ("give us this day our daily bread"). We beg our Father's protection ("deliver us from evil").

These elements of prayer cover the whole range of human conversation: sharing experience, saying thank you, asking for help, crying out in pain, begging forgiveness, expressing love, just spending time together. This is what we do when we get together with our friends. We do the same thing when we get together with God. Prayer takes many forms: mystical prayer, devotional prayer, liturgical prayer, sacred reading, moments of epiphany snatched from our everyday lives.

This is what is meant by the famous Ignatian motto "finding God in all things." "All things" to Ignatius is the whole panoply of human drama—our relationships, our work, our strivings and failures, our hopes and dreams. God can be found in all of it. *Found* does not mean an intellectual exercise . . . . It means engaging God in it, meeting him, dealing with him . . . [similar to] the interacting between family members.

What Is Ignatian Spirituality?

Ignatian Optimism

Ronald Modras

St. Augustine was impressed by the amount of sin in the world; humanity for him was a *massa damnata*. That seems to imply that grace is not only unearned but bestowed sparingly. Ignatius, on the other hand, was impressed by the fact that God spoke to him despite his sinfulness. That implied a liberality to God's giving and forgiving. If God would speak to him, he would speak to anyone. And from a conviction of abundant grace springs what has been called Ignatian optimism. The "contemplation to attain love" is a veritable hymn to grace, aimed at stirring the soul to "profound gratitude" by reflecting on God's generosity as Giver and Gift [233]. If Ignatian spirituality seeks and finds "God in all things," it is because everything is grace.

Ignatian Humanism

Seeking God's Presence in All Things

Ignatius of Loyola

From a letter about the formation of young Jesuits:

They should practice the seeking of God's presence in all things, in their conversations, their walks, in all that they see, taste, hear, understand, in all their actions, since His Divine Majesty is truly in all things by His presence, power, and essence. This kind of meditation, which finds God our Lord in all things, is easier than raising oneself to the consideration of divine truths which are more abstract and which demand something of an effort if we are to keep our attention on them. But this method is an excellent exercise to prepare us for great visitations of our Lord, even in prayers that are rather short.

Letters of Saint Ignatius of Loyola

The Imaginary Boy

Jim Manney

In *Anna Karenina* by Leo Tolstoy, the writer describes the thoughts of a nine-year-old boy: "His father always talked to him—so he felt—as if he were addressing some imaginary boy, one of those that exist in books, but quite unlike him. And he always tried, when he was with his father, to pretend he was that book boy."

These sentences struck me like a thunderclap, and I wondered why. It's hardly a novel insight that we often pretend to be someone other than who we really are, or that people often treat us as someone we're not. I think the passage struck me because it captures in a few sentences the utter futility of an all-too-common human situation. Everybody's playing make-believe. The father has a fantasy of the son. The boy pretends he is that son, knowing that he's not.

Walter Burghardt, SJ, calls prayer "a long, loving look at the real." He writes, "What is real? Reality, is not reducible to some far-off, abstract, intangible God-in-the-sky. Reality is living, pulsing people; reality is fire and ice." Reality is the real boy and the real father. Prayer is an end to the game of let's pretend.

Ignatian Spirituality.com

Where Is Our God in Suffering?

Richard Hauser, SJ

Where is our God in suffering? We Christians do not have a fully satisfying explanation for why the world contains so much suffering. But we have something better: we have the power to deal with the suffering. We know where our God is during suffering. Our God is with us: with the Jewish boy on the gallows, with Ivan Ilyich in sickness, with Job in adversity, with Paul in weakness and persecution, with Jesus in crucifixion—with us in all the senseless accidents and ruptured relationships and interior brokenness of our lives. And we cannot claim to be living a fully Christian life until we believe and live this dimension of the gospel, trusting God's presence and power working through our own "thorns in the flesh," Gethsemanes, and Calvarys. . . .

Our God is with us through the Holy Spirit. To the degree we respond to God's Spirit we live in God, fulfill the promise of our creation, and become conformed to Christ—in good times and in troubled times.

Finding God in Troubled Times

Imagination

Two Ways of Prayerful Imagining
David L. Fleming, SJ

Rules for Imaginative Prayer
Margaret Silf

Lingering over God
Maureen Conroy

What Kind of World Are We Living In?
Chris Lowney

In Unapproachable Light
William J. O'Malley, SJ

The Jesus of the Gospels Becomes *Our* Jesus
David L. Fleming, SJ

God Deals with Us Directly
J. Michael Sparough, SJ; Jim Manney; and Tim Hipskind, SJ

The Movement toward Christ
Howard Gray, SJ

Imagine
Vinita Hampton Wright

Women of Goodness
Gary Smith, SJ

The World as It Really Is
Joseph A. Tetlow, SJ

Sacred Events of Great Significance
John J. English, SJ

This Is Seedtime
Alfred Delp, SJ

Two Ways of Prayerful Imagining

David L. Fleming, SJ

Ignatius presents two ways of imagining in the Spiritual Exercises. The first is demonstrated in a meditation on the mystery of the Incarnation. He asks us to "enter into the vision of God." God is looking down on our turbulent world. We imagine God's concern for the world. We see God intervening by sending Jesus into the maelstrom of life. This type of imagining helps us see things from God's perspective and take on God's qualities of love, compassion, and understanding.

The second method of imagining is to place ourselves fully within a story from the Gospels. We become onlooker-participants . . . Jesus is speaking to a blind man at the side of the road. We feel the Mediterranean sun beating down. We smell the dust kicked up by passersby. We feel the itchy clothing we're wearing, the sweat rolling down our brow, a rumble of hunger. We see the desperation in the blind man's face and hear the wail of hope in his words. We note the irritation of the disciples. Above all we watch Jesus—[his walk and] gestures, the look in his eyes, the expression on his face. We hear him speak the words that are recorded in the Gospel. We imagine other words he might have spoken and other deeds he might have done.

What Is Ignatian Spirituality?

Rules for Imaginative Prayer

Margaret Silf

There are two absolute rules for imaginative prayer: *1) Never moralize or judge yourself; 2) Always respond from your heart and not from your head.* Neither rule is as easy as it sounds. Many of us carry judgmental attitudes toward ourselves, and we are habitually critical of ourselves. We have also been taught to study the Word of God, and of course it's right to do this. But there is a time for recognizing that our heads can never grasp the truths of God, and that our purpose in prayer is not to defend or condemn ourselves or to come up with any kind of analysis or sermon, but simply to respond, from our inmost depths, to what God is sharing with us.

So allow your feelings and your moods to have their say. If you have feelings of tenderness or apprehension or anger in the Gospel scene you're imagining, this tells you about what is happening between you and God at that particular moment. Just as you take notice of how you are feeling and reacting in your human relationships, so, too, your feelings and reactions in your relationship with God are significant, even if they appear to be negative. We often learn more from our negative reactions than from the more comfortable ones.

Inner Compass, adapted

Lingering over God

Maureen Conroy

God's touch, though taking place in a moment of time, lives on within us forever. When we experience God's love, God's self-giving, we are never the same. We may return to some of our old ways of being and acting, but deep down within we are not the same.

We can continue to let an experience of God bear fruit within us by going back to it and lingering over it. Through this remembering, lingering, and reliving process, we open ourselves to God—we allow God to move within us, to touch our hearts again so that our own experiences of God ripple deep within us and can continue to make a difference in our lives.

The Discerning Heart

What Kind of World Are We Living In?

Chris Lowney

The Spiritual Exercises invite us to look at the world as God would see it: "full of people ... so diverse in dress and behavior: some white and others black, some in peace and others at war, some weeping and others laughing, some healthy and others sick, some being born and others dying" (#102, #106). What would God think of the state of our world? What do you think of it?

Why is this mental exercise important? Because facing facts about the world can help us see more clearly how we want to lead our civilization forward. What kind of world are we living in, where is it heading, and what part has each of us played in getting it there? Those big-picture questions typically remain unanswered because so many other concerns tunnel our vision. No future world event seems more consequential than the size of my upcoming raise, and no past injustice seems greater than the money I lost to the coffee vendor who shortchanged me this morning. For an accurate perception of our world, we have to lift our heads a bit higher in order to see a bit farther.

Heroic Living

In Unapproachable Light

William J. O'Malley, SJ

Becoming aware that we have been divinized by Jesus Christ, invited into the Trinity family, is not the same as the self-aggrandizing divinization of Roman emperors. Rather it is a felt realization of the numinous presence of God not only all around us but also within us. God is there all the time, waiting. But, like God's forgiveness, God's will to share the divine aliveness with us can't activate until we invite it. It is the heart-stopping understanding that despite our shortcomings, despite our seeming insignificance to most of those around us, the God who dwells in unapproachable light dwells within us. As he did in a Bethlehem stable.

God: The Oldest Question

The Jesus of the Gospels Becomes *Our* Jesus

David L. Fleming, SJ

To follow Jesus we must know him, and we get to know him through our imagination. Imaginative Ignatian prayer teaches us things about Jesus that we would not learn through scripture study or theological reflection. It allows the person of Christ to penetrate into places that the intellect does not touch. It brings Jesus into our hearts. It engages our feelings. It enflames us with ideals of generous service.

Imaginative prayer makes the Jesus of the Gospels *our* Jesus. It helps us develop a unique and personal relationship with him. We watch Jesus' face. We listen to the way he speaks. We notice how people respond to him. These imaginative details bring us to know Jesus as more than a name or a historical figure in a book. He is a living person. We say what the villagers in John's Gospel told the Samaritan woman: "We have come to know him ourselves, and not just from your report."

What Is Ignatian Spirituality?

God Deals with Us Directly

J. Michael Sparough, SJ; Jim Manney; and Tim Hipskind, SJ

We can trust our experience because God deals with us directly. Ignatius certainly believed that the Church and Scripture are trustworthy teachers of truth and that we need that truth to help us interpret our experience. He also believed that Christians receive spiritual nourishment in the sacraments and in devotional prayer. But he also believed that God communicates directly to each of us. We can have a personal relationship with God. Prayer in the Ignatian mode is essentially a conversation. He warned spiritual directors not to get in the way. "Leave the creator to act immediately with the creature," he wrote.

What's Your Decision?

The Movement toward Christ

Howard Gray, SJ

The *Exercises* represent a kind of spiritual journey, as they invite the one who makes them to consider the foundational truths of Christian life: creation as an act of love, human stewardship of creation, sin and forgiveness, the life and work of Jesus as a paradigm of discipleship, Christ's suffering, death, and resurrection and, finally, the surrender of all human life into the hands of a loving God. The Ignatian take on the Christian journey is to insist that it is a movement, an active progress towards a radical decision to live one's life in harmony with Christ's vision and values. The movement towards Christ is both inward and outward, horizontal and vertical, contemplative and active.

As Leaven in the World

Imagine

Vinita Hampton Wright

What is the most imaginative thing you've ever done?

Who is the most imaginative person you know, and how would you describe that person's life and work? . . . What are your deep desires today? Or, what is your deep dissatisfaction?

Imagination is at the root of creation. What kind of work would you like to create? What kind of workplace? What kind of church? What kind of home?

During the next few days, generate as many ideas as you can about a particular desire or dissatisfaction. Just go crazy, and don't worry about how impractical the ideas are or how unqualified you may be to carry them out. Ask divine imagination to accompany you as you mull over these matters.

Pick something attractive you would like to create, and make steps this week to begin doing just that.

Days of Deepening Friendship

Women of Goodness

Gary Smith, SJ

I have wept with and consoled the Sudanese refugee woman . . . I have buried her after childbirth. I have anointed her as she was dying of some tropical disease. I have given her alms when she has extended her hand, fingers lost to leprosy. I have raced my car over impossible roads to get her to a clinic where she can deliver her baby. I have been with her when she is dying of the shock of a breech birth, a little foot sticking out of her body. I have helped her younger daughters continue with their studies in the face of a cultural attitude that educating a girl child is not necessary. I have fallen in love with the African mother, whose goodness and beauty have left me shaking.

One day, such a mother, Mary Kenyi, came to me. She often came by, asking for a few beans or some grain and sometimes for a blanket. All of her children were killed in the Sudan civil war, along with her husband. I saw her coming toward me and thought, *I wonder what she will be asking for today?* She carried a small plastic bag and handed it to me, giving me a smile that would capture the heart of the most heartless.

In the bag was a gift for me. Three eggs.

They Come Back Singing

The World as It Really Is

Joseph A. Tetlow, SJ

Those who really do know and love [Jesus] will . . . see the suffering of all the people whom God puts in their life and world, and strive with great effort to grieve with them and do whatever they can to alleviate their suffering. Right here is the deepest spiritual root of the impulse to work for peace and justice. Anything less would be an unworthy motive for those who love Jesus Christ.

Jesus' passion brings us to embrace the world as it really is: full of violence and pain. We refuse to let religion and grace become an easy analgesic, buffering us from the real sufferings around us. Instead, we embrace whatever suffering comes into our lives as no longer senseless. Our suffering has a meaning in "the language of the cross" (1 Corinthians 1:18). We join the sufferings of the crucified Christ, the sufferings of humankind that he chose to embrace. We cling to Jesus, to "a Christ who is the power and the wisdom of God" (1 Corinthians 1:24). When we do less, we are using our faith in Christ as a pain pill.

Making Choices in Christ

Sacred Events of Great Significance

John J. English, SJ

The contemplative method of prayer can be understood easily by noting the power of memory and imagination in ordinary life. It is not difficult for most people to fall into a reverie. They become oblivious to what surrounds them and are caught up in the scene or circumstances of former events that made a deep impression on them. They hear what was said, see the actions, gestures, and expressions of those involved, and experience anew the mysterious meaning of what happened. It matters little when or where it took place—New York, Vancouver, or Paris. The person's whole self is preoccupied with that arresting moment. This is what memory and imagination can do.

In Ignatian contemplation we form the habit of losing ourselves . . . in sacred events of great significance. After some initial practice, we learn how to stay with the scene and its actions, to relax in the presence of those who speak and move, and to open ourselves without reserve to what occurs, so that we may receive a deep impression of the event's mysterious meaning.

Spiritual Freedom

This Is Seedtime

Alfred Delp, SJ

One thing is becoming gradually clear—I must surrender myself completely. This is seedtime, not harvest. God sows the seed and some time or other he will do the reaping. The one thing I must do is to make sure the seed falls on fertile ground. And I must arm myself against the pain and depression that sometimes almost defeat me. If this is the way God has chosen—and everything indicates that it is—then I must willingly and without rancor make it my way. May others at some future time find it possible to have a better and happier life because we died in this hour of trial.

With Bound Hands

Loving God

What It Takes to Change
Paul Coutinho, SJ

Our Way of Proceeding
Pedro Arrupe, SJ

No Commonplace Achievements
Chris Lowney

Becoming Aware of God's Desire for You
Maureen Conroy

Sin Is Revealed in Love
George A. Aschenbrenner, SJ

Inflamed with Love of God
Ignatius of Loyola

More Than Ever
Pedro Arrupe, SJ

A Sense of Reverence

Gerald M. Fagin, SJ

I remember standing on top of a mesa ten thousand feet high overlooking what seemed to be hundreds of miles of fertile land. I experienced amazement, silence, vastness, expansiveness, gift. I felt a sense of wonder that God had almost done too much and thus created out of the sheer joy of creating and sharing goodness.

We feel such things often—in the countless stars on a clear night, before a work of art, at the birth of a child, at the moment of dying of a loved one. These contemplative experiences draw us closer to God even as we feel small and unworthy. . . .

Ignatius believed that anyone who prayerfully considers the basic truth that we are created out of love by a transcendent God of holiness will grow in a sense of reverence. We will have a deepened sense of the sacredness of all things if we think of everything as continually being called and sustained by God. We will stand in awe not just before sunsets and mountains, flowers and trees, but also, and especially, before every person we meet. Reverence is a disposition of heart that allows us to live before the beauty and goodness of every creature and the God who made them. In Ignatian terminology, reverence will enable us to find God in all things.

Putting on the Heart of Christ

Nothing Is More Practical Than Finding God

Pedro Arrupe, SJ

Nothing is more practical than
finding God, than
falling in Love
in a quite absolute, final way.
What you are in love with,
what seizes your imagination, will affect everything.
It will decide what will get you out of bed in the
      morning,
what you do with your evenings,
how you spend your weekends,
what you read, whom you know,
what breaks your heart,
and what amazes you with joy and gratitude.
Fall in Love, stay in love,
and it will decide everything.

Ignatian Spirituality.com

Be Grateful

Chris Lowney

Ignatius of Loyola reminded us that we ourselves are one of this world's greatest marvels. Look at the world with gratitude and awe, but look at yourself with the same attitude. We are more talented, gifted, and resourceful than we ever consider. In one spiritual exercise, Ignatius counsels us to bask gratefully in the sheer wonder of our being by considering "how God dwells . . . also in myself, giving me existence, life, sensation, and intelligence; and, even further, making me his temple, since I am created as a likeness and image of the Divine Majesty" (#235).

Be grateful for your talents and gifts because they are the raw material out of which you will conceive and shape your life's purpose. Whoever we are, whatever our circumstances, we can, as Archbishop Oscar Romero once put it, "do something and do it very well," whether that is raising children, teaching them to read, keeping the streets safe for them, creating dignified jobs for their parents, erecting buildings that will safely shelter them, or thinking and praying benevolent thoughts for their future.

Be grateful because gratitude is what energizes and motivates us to pursue great purpose.

Heroic Living

Freedom to Show Compassion

Paul Coutinho, SJ

Let us pray for the grace of being compassionate. In a living relationship with God, we are connected to and affected by what happens to *anyone* in life. With an infinitely big God, color fades away, creed fades away. Good and bad fade away. We can see beyond color, beyond religion, beyond a person being morally good or bad. As Jesus said, "I condemn the sin but never the sinner." The sinner is also me. I praise virtue, but again that person who is virtuous is also me. This is when I know I am in a living relationship with the Divine: when I can relate to another person's interior being, and I care about the world as much as I care about myself.

When I put this case to my students at the university, one of them challenged, "So in compassion you do not have any freedom!" But as I told this student, freedom comes with response plus ability. The ability to respond is freedom. In charity, my ability to respond is limited to the people I choose to help, the time I choose to give, and the price I'm willing to pay. In compassion, the ability to respond is total.

How Big Is Your God?

Godseed

Margaret Silf

As Christians, we talk about God as being both immanent (present to us, individually and collectively, in our hearts and in our human experience) and transcendent (utterly beyond our reach or imagination, totally "other" and without limits). My Godseed is nothing less than the immanent God at rest in my heart, waiting to be expressed in an act of germination, of resurrection. . . .

We can notice moments when we seem to be in contact with something, or someone, beyond ourselves. We know that something has happened that is different from the normal run of our daily lives. We might feel as if we have been touched by God. It could have happened through intense communion with nature or in a human relationship, in a moment of deep insight that seemed to come from beyond ourselves, or perhaps in a sudden clarity that showed us the way forward in a particular situation.

When these moments happen, we could say that God has "taken root." That touch of Life will, if we allow it, penetrate down through the layers of our experience until it reaches the center. There, the transcendent God will join with the immanent God locked up, like a seed, in our hearts, and something new will grow from that union.

Inner Compass

The Gratitude List

Jim Manney

A friend of mine was stuck in traffic in New York City late on a summer Friday afternoon. He was really stuck—sitting in his car on a narrow east-west cross street in Manhattan, going nowhere. He grew impatient, then angry. After a while, he started to think about how pitiful his life was. His friends were smarter, wealthier, happier than he was. He hadn't accomplished anything significant. He was stuck in life, just as he was stuck in traffic.

Then he called a friend and asked for help. The guy said, "If you're just sitting there in traffic, make a gratitude list." So my friend pulled out a notebook and pen and made a list of all the things he was grateful for. A few were big things—family, friends, job—but most of them were little things. The weekend coming up. An excellent novel he was reading. A compliment from his boss the previous day. An exhilarating jog along the East River that morning. His comfortable car. Soon his mood lifted. The exercise in gratitude restored balance to his thinking. It wasn't a trick. My friend saw that his life really was full of good things. Gratitude was the truth.

Ignatian Spirituality.com

A Rush of Awe

George A. Aschenbrenner, SJ

As a being created by God, you are involved in a relationship with the Creator that gleams with a moment-by-moment immediacy. Creation is not some fatalistic scenario within which you rudely awaken, nor your own act of self-determination, nor an ancient act that long ago began the process of being. No, creation has the immediacy of constant present tense. An awareness of this immediacy at any moment can startle your soul and excite your heart in a rush of awe even now as you read these words—and as I pen them. Being created, being enlivened breath by breath unto a final breath that lasts forever: this awareness, like electricity coursing through your person, rouses concrete desires in your heart and invites your free co-creative cooperation. Words on a page fall far short of the actual experience, whose taste and appreciation require time, inner quiet, and prayerful reflection.

Stretched for Greater Glory

The Most Abominable of Sins

Ignatius of Loyola

It seems to me in the light of the Divine Goodness, although others may think differently, that ingratitude is the most abominable of sins and that it should be detested in the sight of our Creator and Lord by all of His creatures who are capable of enjoying His divine and everlasting glory. For it is a forgetting of the graces, benefits, and blessings received. As such it is the cause, beginning, and origin of all sins and misfortunes. On the contrary, the grateful acknowledgment of blessings and gifts received is loved and esteemed not only on earth but in heaven.

Letters of Saint Ignatius of Loyola

What It Takes to Change

Paul Coutinho, SJ

Without the willingness to be spiritually challenged, we cannot and will not change. Without the will to give up whatever is asked of us in order to meet a bigger God, we find that our understanding and experience of the Divine cannot and will not grow. . . .

God took Abraham through the desert, and if you have the will to follow, he'll take you through the desert too. The desert represents a place of purification and pure encounter with God, with no obstacles or distractions. The desert is the place where you will experience the naked truth of who you are—the image and likeness of God, the divine breath. While you're in the desert, God may come for your beloved Isaac and ask you to sacrifice him. Isaac was Abraham's son and God's own gift and promise to him.

Do you still want to know God? Do you still want to see the face of the Divine? Do you have the will to experience your own spiritual and divine identity and become a channel of divine blessing?

How Big Is Your God?

Our Way of Proceeding

Pedro Arrupe, SJ

Lord, meditating on "our way of proceeding," I have discovered that the ideal way of *our* way of acting is your way of acting.

Give me that *sensus Christi* that I may feel with your feelings, with the sentiments of your heart, which basically are love for your Father and love for all men and women.

Teach me how to be compassionate to the suffering, to the poor, the blind, the lame, and the lepers.

Teach us your way so that it becomes our way today, so that we may come closer to the great ideal of Saint Ignatius: to be companions of Jesus, collaborators in the work of redemption.

Other Apostolates Today

No Commonplace Achievements

Chris Lowney

When Loyola informed Portuguese Jesuits that "no commonplace achievement will satisfy the great obligations you have of excelling," he created heroic expectations that could be met only through change and innovation on a dramatic scale. By way of illustration, imagine any modern corporate setting. The manager who sets an expense reduction target of 10 percent gets his team wondering where to buy cheaper pencils: 10 percent means safe, mainstream thinking. An expense reduction target of 40 percent, however, is "no commonplace achievement" but a *heroically* ambitious target that requires outside-the-box thinking. With this goal, no one is thinking about cheaper pencils anymore; it's time to conceive radically new ways of doing things. So it wasn't enough for Jesuit teams in Paraguay to advocate marginally better treatment of indigenous people within the *encomienda* system; they rejected the whole system to establish the radically new reduction model. The tradition of thinking outside the box began when Loyola himself jettisoned the centuries-old model of religious life to invent a completely new kind of religious company.

Heroic Leadership

Becoming Aware of God's Desire for You

Maureen Conroy

Spend time looking at God. Who is God for you now? How is God present with you at this moment?

What is God's desire for you like? Listen to God express this desire.

Jesus said: "How often I have yearned to gather you, as a mother bird gathers her young under her wings. . . ." (Mt. 23:37). How would you image or express God's desire for you as you are sensing it now?

Let yourself feel God's desire for you. How do you feel as you get in touch with this desire? joyful? grateful? fearful?

Share this feeling with God. Ask for a greater awareness of and openness to God's desire for you.

The Discerning Heart

Sin Is Revealed in Love

George A. Aschenbrenner, SJ

Sin has an objectivity beyond your own awareness. "Sin is a frightful ingratitude on the part of the creature toward his or her all-loving Creator," as Cusson presents it. To let this objective reality pierce through the net of rationalization that we use to overlook or justify our sin takes time. It also presumes that your relationship with your loving Creator is still alive in your heart, because, finally, it is the presence of God's gracious love that reveals your sin. So often in the past, unhealthy, shameful influences have shaken the finger of guilt in your face regarding sin. Here the experience is quite different. Within your growing awareness of sin, something profoundly personal and hopeful is at work. The fire of God's love is inviting you insistently into the deep glow of peace and the radiant energy of salvation in Christ Jesus. Your own memory and willpower cannot produce this revelation. Without a lively sense of God's love, this revelation of sin is not possible.

Stretched for Greater Glory

Inflamed with Love of God

Ignatius of Loyola

I call it consolation when an interior movement is aroused in the soul, by which it is inflamed with love of its Creator and Lord, and as a consequence, can love no creature on the face of the earth for its own sake, but only in the Creator of them all. It is likewise consolation when one sheds tears that move to the love of God, whether it be because of sorrow for sins, or because of the sufferings of Christ our Lord, or for any other reason that is immediately directed to the praise and service of God. Finally, I call consolation every increase of faith, hope, and love, and all interior joy that invites and attracts to what is heavenly and to the salvation of one's soul by filling it with peace and quiet in its Creator and Lord.

The Spiritual Exercises of St. Ignatius

More Than Ever

Pedro Arrupe, SJ

Pedro Arrupe composed this prayer after he suffered a debilitating stroke, the effects of which he patiently endured for the final ten years of his life.

More than ever, I now find myself in the hands of God.
This is what I have wanted all my life, from my youth.

But now there is a difference:
the initiative is entirely with God.

It is indeed a profound spiritual experience
to know and feel myself so totally in God's hands.

33rd General Congregation of the Society of Jesus

Prayer

The Spirituality of CPR
Edward Peck

A Prayer for Spiritual Freedom
John A. Veltri, SJ

Why Was I Delivered from Death?
Gary Smith, SJ

God Wants Our Friendship

William A. Barry, SJ

I maintain that God—out of the abundance of divine relational life, not any need for us—desires humans into existence for the sake of friendship.

This thesis may sound strange, because it runs counter to much teaching about God. I questioned it myself when I first began to think it through. . . . I have used the analogy of a personal relationship between two people to describe the developing relationship between God and us. But the notion that God wants our friendship did not easily follow. Whenever it reared its head, I shrugged it off as a fancy not to be taken seriously. . . .

But as my own relationship with God has deepened and I have listened to people talk about how God relates to them, I have become convinced that the best analogy for the relationship God wants with us is friendship. I began to use this kind of language in talks and articles and found that it resonated with others. I hope that you will find similar resonance and will trust your experience more fully. I can think of nothing that would please me more than to hear that you, and many others, have come to find God "better than he's made out to be," as my Irish mother once put it.

A Friendship Like No Other

Time Taken Out

Margaret Silf

Prayer is time taken out of the linear journey of our days, and it is also our most profound reality. When we pray, we move inward to our God center. Then we move out again . . . to our situation in the world. This movement into the center and out again brings about an act of transformation. This is not to say that we will come out of prayer transfigured, like Jesus on the mountain (though our prayer experience may sometimes be dramatic). Nothing so spectacular! Usually there is a subtle, gentle, almost indiscernible change in our way of being that will carry its healing, changing power out through the layers of our lived experience and infuse the Where of our lives with its Kingdom values. This happens every time we pray, whether we are aware of it or not.

Inner Compass

Wash Me with Your Precious Blood

Peter Canisius, SJ

See, O merciful God, what return
I, your thankless servant, have made
for the innumerable favors
and the wonderful love you have shown me!
What wrongs I have done, what good left undone!
Wash away, I beg you, these faults and stains
with your precious blood, most kind Redeemer,
and make up for my poverty by applying your merits.
Give me the protection I need to amend my life.
I give and surrender myself wholly to you,
and offer you all I possess,
with the prayer that you bestow your grace on me,
so that I may be able to devote and employ
all the thinking power of my mind
and the strength of my body in your holy service,
who are God blessed forever and ever. Amen.

Hearts on Fire

Prayer Works

Tim Muldoon

Skeptics claim that prayer does nothing; you don't always get what you pray for, and the best it can do is make you feel good. Yet I think that view is myopic. We learn to pray over a lifetime, in a manner similar to the way we learn to enter relationships. Just as a child doesn't always get what she asks for ("candy!" if you're an eight year old whose father is writing at this moment), neither does the petitioner immediately get a handy response from the "vending-machine God" (pop in prayer, wait for nifty result).

What I see, looking back over years of my life, is a deepening of my capacity to love. Prayer has challenged me to take a long look at what I desire out of life, and what I am willing to risk for love. It has made me much more savvy about the way my feelings work. Following Ignatius's advice about feelings in the Spiritual Exercises has made me back away from giving too much credence to any particular feeling at any particular time, without seeing it against the backdrop of my deeper desires and discerning its possible origins.

Prayer works because God is working, and my prayer is that my own work may be a participation in God's work,

Ignatian Spirituality.com, adapted

Distractions during Prayer

Kevin O'Brien, SJ

If you can, simply acknowledge the distracting thought and let it go. Sometimes, however, what at first seems like a distraction offers an opportunity for a graced encounter with God. Thus, if the distracting thought continues, then carefully discern whether it's really a distraction or something you need to pray about. In the course of a retreat in daily life, things happen at home, at work, or in relationships that beg for prayerful reflection. We should not hesitate to pray over the "scripture of our lives" if we think that God is trying to get our attention through what we initially thought was a distraction. . . .

Sometimes it can seem that nothing is happening, but deep down, God might be stirring up something—we just haven't realized it yet. As you grow in the habit of prayer, avoid the temptation to judge or rate your prayer: "Today was good prayer; yesterday was just OK." (Imagine rating each time you spent with a friend or loved one!) God can put anything to good use, even distractions and preoccupations.

The Ignatian Adventure

Four Reasons to Avoid Extreme Prayer Practices

Ignatius of Loyola

From a letter to a Jesuit community that had embraced very rigorous prayer practices.

The first is that God is not really served in the long run, as the horse worn out in the first days does not as a rule finish the journey, and thus it happens that someone must be found to care for it.

Second, gains that are made through this excessive eagerness are not usually kept. Not only diminished, but it may be the cause of a fall: "And he that is hasty with his feet shall stumble"; and if he stumbles, the further he falls, the greater the danger, for he will not stop until he has reached the bottom of the ladder.

Third, there is the danger of being careless about overloading the vessel. There is danger, of course, in sailing it empty, as it can then be tossed about on the waves of temptation. But there is also danger of so overloading it as to cause it to sink.

Fourth, it can happen that, in crucifying the old man, the new man is also crucified and thus made unable through weakness to practice virtue.

Letters of Saint Ignatius of Loyola

The Whole Self in Prayer

Vinita Hampton Wright

How are emotions involved in your prayer? Can you express them, or do you repress them, especially anger and hurt?

How does your physical self relate to your conversation with God? How aware are you of what your body is doing when you pray? How have you involved your body in prayer? Do you ever sing when you pray? Have you tried drawing pictures or coloring? How might you do prayer more visually?

Get into a comfortable position. Take several slow, deep breaths. Now, close your eyes and be silent for a few moments. If worries intrude or you keep thinking of things you need to do, write them down and set them aside and go back to a quiet mind.

And then imagine yourself in prayer. See yourself walking to a specific place and praying there. Observe what you do with your body while praying. Note the expression on your face. Listen to the words of prayer that come out of your mouth—or, if you are praying silently, hear the unspoken thoughts.

When the prayer in your imagination is finished, reflect on what you witnessed. Write down your observations. Talk with God about them.

Days of Deepening Friendship

Three Little Ways of Praying

Joseph A. Tetlow, SJ

The First Little Way of Praying: Recall the commandments or any list such as the Cardinal Virtues or the Capital Sins. Take each in turn, consider the beautiful divine invitation it expresses, and ask yourself how you are living it out. Thank your Creator and Lord for all your good and beg God to make up for your lacks and failures.

The Second Little Way of Praying: Pray any prayer you know—the Our Father, Apostles' Creed, Hail Mary—and consider it one word at a time, savoring each word until you are finished with it, and then moving to the next. Thus, you would wonder what it means that you call the Father "Our," and how you live out that meaning; then when you are done with that word, move on to "Father," and so the "Amen."

The Third Little Way of Praying: Pray any prayer you know rhythmically, saying one word or phrase each time you breathe in or take a step walking or hear the subway wheels hit a track divider.

Of course, in any way of praying you begin coming to self-concentration in God, ask the Lord for what you want, and end by talking with your Creator and Lord.

Choosing Christ in the World

The Spirituality of CPR

Edward Peck

"Look, listen, and feel." These are the basic instructions of any CPR course. We know from experience that to help a person who appears to be in physical distress, it is important first to see what is really going on before intervening, lest one do more harm than good. Let's look more closely at the caring act of providing CPR to see what spiritual lessons we might find. . . .

Paying attention to what is really going on and checking things out with all the tools at our disposal are important lessons for all of life, but particularly for the spiritual life. . . . Because things are not always as they seem, it is important to check things out before trying to fix, change, or "improve" something in our lives.

Given the hustle and bustle and demands of everyday life, I wonder if I am attentive enough to what is really going on in my spiritual life. I wonder, too, if I might need to be shaken up a bit to find out if I am merely sleeping or if I am really out of it. "Eddie, Eddie, are you all right?" I wonder further: What about my spiritual pulse? How would I check it? Am I "breathing"? Does the Spirit's breath cause my chest to rise from within?

Ignatian Spirituality.com

A Prayer for Spiritual Freedom

John A. Veltri, SJ

This prayer is frequently used by Jesuits to begin classes and meetings.

O Spirit of God, we ask you to help orient
all our actions by your inspirations,
and carry them on by your gracious assistance,
that every prayer and work of ours
may always begin from you
and through you be happily ended.

Orientations

Why Was I Delivered from Death?

Gary Smith, SJ

Reflection after life-saving emergency surgery in Africa

How can I explain the extraordinary way in which I was delivered from death? A break, a coincidence, or Providence? Can I dare consider that God acts personally in the direction of my life? Ultimately, I fall back on the fact that there are movements, people, and events in my life that I could never have created myself. . . .

This is not triumphant self-absorption; it is simply standing before the evidence and truth of my life. If God is involved in my life, then God is involved in my life—period. God's love is palpable, transparent, unyielding, inescapable. . . .

What about all the people who do not find God acting personally in their lives? Insofar as I can accompany them and help them understand the Love that impels and surrounds me, I will. If I have been taken care of, then it is to allow me to bring Love once again into the universe . . . by my touch, by my prayer, by my suffering, by my presence. I am too old now to argue with anyone about the validity of this compelling force in my life and the way I see it. One finally has to take oneself into one's arms and say, *This is who I am, and this is the Love that calls me into existence.*

They Come Back Singing

Work

Make a Good Effort and Leave the Rest to Him
Ignatius of Loyola

Magis-Driven Leaders
Chris Lowney

Doing the Will of God
Kevin O'Brien, SJ

Looking at the World as God's Project

Tim Muldoon

Looking at the world as God's project has some powerful implications.

- It emphasizes the radical human freedom with which God has created us, and the passion God brings to persuading us to help God create a kingdom of goodness, truth, and beauty.

- It allows us to see human evil as getting in the way, but not abolishing the project. Grace is still everywhere: God is still laboring at the project even when people abandon it.

- It helps us understand what prayer is all about: the practice of discerning the project in all its intricate dimensions, and aligning our desires with God's desires.

- It helps us see our very selves as part of that project, and others as well.

- It reminds us that the project is at once about the "now"—every hair on my head—and the "forever"—the whole of human history, cosmic history, and eternity.

- It is a reminder that our halting attempts at love are "practice" and that as we become more adept at love we contribute more and more to the unfolding of the project, increasingly awed by the way God uses our small selves to paint and sculpt the world with great beauty.

Ignatian Spirituality.com

Don't Shun Small Works

Ignatius of Loyola

We should never postpone a good work, no matter how small it may be, with the thought of later doing something greater. It is a very common temptation of the enemy to be always placing before us the perfection of things to come and bring us to make little of the present.

Let us all persevere in the vocation to which God calls us, and not make our first loyalty an empty word. For the enemy is wont to tempt those in the desert with thoughts of dealing with the neighbor and improving him, and to those who are helping the neighbor he will propose the great perfection of the desert and solitary life. Thus he lays hold of what is far off to prevent us from taking advantage of what is at hand.

Letters of Saint Ignatius of Loyola

Creating with God

Lyn Holley Doucet

As we look around our beautiful world, we see the God of creativity. This God did not content himself with creating one pink flower; he created thousands. He created not one lizard, but hundreds of types of lizards; not one cookie-cutter person, but billions of unique souls. Truly, God delights in variety, in creativity, in creation. And God delights when we create. This I believe with all my heart. As Ignatius said, "These desires [to serve] do not come from yourself, but are given to you by the Lord." God calls us to be cocreators in the world that has already begun.

The evil one will tell us over and over that we have nothing to offer. We can easily lead colorless lives of safety and depression if we allow these voices to overcome us. As Ignatius told Teresa Rejadell, "He draws you away from greater service and from our own greater peace of mind."

A Healing Walk with St. Ignatius

The Purpose of Learning
Is to Serve Others

Ignatius of Loyola

Experience teaches us that many great and learned men, because of their lack of training, have to keep their learning to themselves and are balked of the main purpose for which they should have acquired their learning, which was to be of benefit to their neighbor. If there are others who do share the benefits of their learning, it is not with that authority and success they would have if they were as able to explain themselves as they are to understand, and to throw as much light upon their ideas when they give them forth as they had within their minds to understand these ideas themselves. This I think can be seen even in scholastic doctors. For if a part of their shrewd and learned acquisitions could be exchanged for a skillful way of explaining the remainder, they could with what remained achieve a more widespread good than they now do with all their learning.

Letters of Saint Ignatius of Loyola

Work Gives God Glory

Gerard Manley Hopkins, SJ

When a man is in God's grace and free from mortal sin, then everything that he does, as long as there is no sin in it, gives God glory. . . . It is not only prayer that gives God glory but work. Smiting on an anvil, sawing a beam, whitewashing a wall, driving horses, sweeping, scouring, everything gives God some glory if being in his grace you do it as your duty. . . . To lift up the hands in prayer gives God glory, but a man with a dung fork in his hand, a woman with a slop pail, gives him glory too. He is so great that all things give him glory if you mean they should.

Poems and Prose

A Task, Not a List of Truths

William A. Barry, SJ

Jesus did not leave us a list of truths to affirm, but a task to carry out. We must try to discern in our time and place how God wants us to live our lives in this world in tune with God's Spirit, the one divine action at work in this universe. This is what the discernment of spirits is all about. Followers of Jesus have been given a task to carry out and the means to do it. Impelled by God's Spirit, they must try to live in this world with the conviction that with the life, death, and resurrection of Jesus all the needful has been done, that God has won the victory he intends. Our task, therefore, is to follow the prompting of the Spirit, who has been poured out in our hearts, to follow the way of Jesus, the way of peace, of love, of the cross. We discern the spirits in order to act as followers of Jesus, as believers. Every act of discernment is an act of faith in what God has done in Jesus of Nazareth and continues to do through the indwelling of God.

Spirit, Style, Story

Washing Feet

Jim Manney

In the foot-washing ceremony of Holy Thursday, everyone in our congregation had their feet washed and washed others' feet. You sat down at the basin and had your feet washed. Then you put your socks and shoes on, knelt down, and washed the feet of the next person in line.

Standing in line I was anxious about how my feet would look, glad I had clean socks on, concerned to do the deed properly when my turn came. It wasn't the incredulity the apostles felt when Jesus insisted that he wash their feet, but it was perhaps a small taste of it. It didn't feel *right*. . . . Not the kind of thing that's supposed to happen in church. But that's the point, isn't it? . . . [Jesus] made a dramatic gesture of humble service—a dirty, disagreeable service that slaves did. Over their objections, he said, "Go and do likewise."

Most of the work of the Spiritual Exercises is an effort to answer the question: *What do I really want?* When we know that, we know what God wants. One sure sign of authentic, God-given desire is desire that is directed toward others rather than ourselves. I knew this as an idea, in an abstract way. But when I washed the feet of a stranger on Holy Thursday, I *knew* it.

Ignatian Spirituality.com

Vocation in Broader Terms

James Martin, SJ

More recently, the notion of vocation has been understood in broader terms, applicable not simply to those who are ordained or who take religious vows, but to everyone. Some are called to be priests and sisters and brothers, to be sure, but others are called to be husbands and wives, fathers and mothers, as well as lawyers, doctors, scientist, artists—and actors, directors, playwrights, set designers, lighting designers, and costume designers. At the heart of the modern understanding of vocation is discovering our individual spiritual path and becoming the person we are meant to be.

Contemporary spiritual writers suggest that the seeds of one's vocation are found most easily in one's desires. Understanding our desires and hopes is a way to discover what we are meant to do and who we are meant to be. In his book, *Letting God Come Close*, Jesuit priest William A. Barry . . . spends an entire chapter on the role of desire in the spiritual life. He advises spiritual directors, pastoral counselors, and retreat directors to pay attention to this key aspect of the heart. Retreat directors, Barry says, "do their most important work when they help [others] to discover what they really want."

A Jesuit Off-Broadway

Make a Good Effort and Leave the Rest to Him

Ignatius of Loyola

If one is involved in much business, even though his intention be good and holy, he must make up his mind to do what he can, without afflicting himself if he cannot do all that he wishes; let him do all that a man ought to do who follows the dictate of a good conscience. If other things permit, you must have patience and not think that God our Lord requires what man cannot accomplish, nor that He wishes you to be cast down. And if one satisfies God, what difference does it make whether he satisfies men? There is no need to wear yourself out, but make a competent and sufficient effort, and leave the rest to Him who can do all He pleases.

Letters of Saint Ignatius of Loyola

Magis-Driven Leaders

Chris Lowney

Heroism begins with each person considering, internalizing, and shaping his or her mission. Whether one works within a large organization or alone, no mission is motivating until it is personal. And it is sustainable only when one makes the search for *magis* a reflexive, daily habit. A *magis*-driven leader is not content to go through the motions or settle for the status quo but is restlessly inclined to look for something more, something greater. Instead of wishing circumstances were different, *magis*-driven leaders either make them different or make the most of them. Instead of waiting for golden opportunities, they find the gold in the opportunities at hand.

Heroes lift themselves up and make themselves greater by pursuing something greater than their self-interest. Our classic heroic role models often do so through extraordinary bravery at uniquely critical moments. But heroism is not limited to these rare and privileged opportunities. They are also heroes who demonstrate the courage, nobility, and greatness of heart to pursue a personal sense of *magis*, to remain pointed toward goals that enhance them as people.

Heroic Leadership

Doing the Will of God

Kevin O'Brien, SJ

Traditionally, the church speaks of "finding" or "doing" the will of God. Such expressions recognize that God is our creator and that God's wisdom surpasses our own. The will of God, however, is not simply something imposed on us from the outside. Because we are created in the image of God, God is present to us at the deepest core of our being. We thus can discern the will of God in *our* deepest desires; this is Ignatius's novel insight. The Exercises help us sort through superficial and fleeting desires and tap into deep, holy longings. God's desires for us and our deepest desires are, in the end, not opposed but are one and the same.

The Ignatian Adventure

Contemplation in Action

Review of the Day for Managers
Paul Brian Campbell, SJ

AMDG
Kirk Roberts

Human Ingenuity or Divine Providence?
Why Not Both?
Chris Lowney

The Hinterland Becomes the Heartland
Margaret Silf

The World Is Our Home

Ronald Modras

Seeking and finding God in all things, Iñigo and his Jesuit companions went where they saw needs. They would ask the pope to send them where he saw the greatest needs. And they would elicit the assistance of laymen and laywomen to help them in their response to those needs. "The world is our home," said Jerónimo Nadal, Iñigo's close associate and someone he credited with truly understanding what the *Spiritual Exercises* is all about. With the world as their home, Jesuits and those who shared their spirituality (the "extended Ignatian family") more often than not found themselves where the people and their needs were most numerous—in city centers. Serving people anywhere in the world and finding God there, Ignatius—again to cite Nadal—became a "contemplative in action." The phrase has become a classic expression of the Ignatian spiritual ideal.

Ignatian Humanism

Mary at the Annunciation

Vinita Hampton Wright

Mary's conversation with Gabriel is a wonderful example of what prayer truly is: our response to God's voice. This wasn't simply a matter of Gabriel telling Mary what would happen. By including Mary's detailed response, the Gospel writer implies that she had a choice. It was her body, after all. She was the one who must figure out a way to tell Joseph and her parents what was happening, and who would have to wait in faith while Joseph planned to break their engagement, before the angel spoke to him too. . . . She would give birth far from her mother and the midwife, surrounded by farm animals. She and Joseph and the child would live as refugees in another country. They would watch their son grow into his manhood and feel his way toward a destiny neither of them understood. . . .

Mary may have never conversed with Gabriel again, but . . . her life was one long prayer, a continuous response to the unfolding of God's action. Luke's Gospel says that she prayed through pondering, holding things deep in her heart. Sometimes I'm sure her conversation with the Divine included tears and waiting. When all we do is sit in the room, quiet and weary, waiting and wondering, we are praying in a way that moves far beyond words and reason.

Days of Deepening Friendship

We Are Alive in the Present Moment

Chris Lowney

[Our examen] teaches us, above all, to live in the present. Our days typically unfurl in frenzied preoccupation with the next meeting to attend, errands to be done, dinner to be prepared, and a hundred other tasks that crowd an efficient day. The monk Thich Nhat Hanh points out that we humans are great at planning and willing to sacrifice today to save for cars and houses tomorrow, "but we have difficulty remembering that we are alive in the present moment, the only moment there is for us to be alive." So he exhorts us to the Buddhist practice of mindfulness, being fully and consciously aware (or mindful) of the present moment. The examen, by briefly pulling us out of our daily maelstrom, can help reorient us to the present. When we get it right, as Thich Nhat Hanh puts it, "Every breath we take, every step we make, can be filled with peace, joy, and serenity."

Learn from the past; envision the future; live in the present. It's a challenging life model to master, but the examen helps us do so.

Heroic Living

The True Center Is Indestructible

Margaret Silf

One Christmas while we were away on vacation, our home was burgled. The intruders ransacked every cupboard, including those in a quiet room that we use for prayer and for days of retreat. Some weeks later, this experience returned to me in prayer, and I was surprised to find that in this room I felt no sense of invasion, even though I knew that hostile strangers had searched through its cupboards. Nothing of their spirit lingered in the room. Then my prayer itself seemed to reassure me that there could be no invasion, no threat in such a place, even if they had stripped the room, because what was truly present there—the spirit of the place—was indestructible, and therefore had no need of arms or defenses.

But that prayer wasn't really about the prayer room. It was about my own inner room, my own reality, my Who center, my true center. It was about that heart of me where I feel utterly vulnerable because there are no defenses there. And there are no defenses there because none are needed. I have no need to defend my Who center because, whatever is done to it, it is indestructible, just as God himself is indestructible.

Inner Compass

A School of Prayer

Kevin O'Brien, SJ

The Exercises are a school of prayer. The two primary forms of praying taught in the Exercises are meditation and contemplation. In *meditation*, we use our intellect to wrestle with basic principles that guide our life. Reading Scripture, we pray over words, images, and ideas. We engage our memory to appreciate the activity of God in our life. Such insights into who God is and who we are before God allow our hearts to be moved.

Contemplation is more about feeling than thinking. Contemplation often stirs the emotions and inspires deep, God-given desires. In contemplation, we rely on our imaginations to place ourselves in a setting from the Gospels or in a scene proposed by Ignatius. Scripture has a central place in the Exercises because it is the revelation of who God is, particularly in Jesus Christ, and of what God does in our world. *In the Exercises, we pray with Scripture; we do not study it.* Although Scripture study is central to any believer's faith, we leave for another time extended biblical exegesis and theological investigation.

The Ignatian Adventure

God Doesn't Care How You Look

Maureen McCann Waldron

"Could you live your everyday life in just six pieces of clothing?" is the question behind a website called *Six Items or Less.* People around the world volunteered to wear only six items of clothing for a month, at work and at home. People wrote about their six choices, how they used them, and how other people reacted to them wearing the same clothes all month.

The astonishing part of this experiment: Virtually no one noticed. People wrote that no one realized they were wearing only six items of clothing over and over again. Wives and husbands both wrote that not even the spouses noticed it. It makes me wonder about the image we try to project to the world and to those around us—and how little it really means.

Do I put off coming before God until I can fix myself up? *I'll really get into my relationship with God when work isn't so busy, or when life is less hectic or my kids are more settled. When I am holier. As soon as I stop being so impatient with other people.* I have to learn over and over again that God is waiting for me and loving me. God is incredibly joyful when I finally put aside the six things I think I need to do or be and just open my heart.

Ignatian Spirituality.com

Shared Silence

Tim Muldoon

During a meeting with spiritual directors, an older Jesuit remarked that those who shared the long retreat—thirty days in silence—emerge as lifelong friends, even without having spoken to each other. I believe I understand why. Contemplating the mystery of God in silence is like gazing together at the transfigured Jesus. Sharing such a gaze—beholding God's mystery together—changes you.

What a beautiful metaphor for what lovers do. I have often quoted Antoine de Saint-Exupéry: "Love does not consist in gazing at each other, but in looking outward together in the same direction." I wonder if some lovers have lost the sense that there is anything else to look at besides each other and that when they become bored they move on.

The promise of love is like the promise of a shared pilgrimage: that of moving together toward God, and therefore toward the source of love. Only with such a hopeful promise can couples weather the inevitable storms of pilgrimage. And only with such a promise can one sustain hope, desire, joy—even during periods when one is unhappy. On the other hand, when one is happy one can appreciate it but not get too caught up in it; what matters is not the weather but the progress of the pilgrimage.

Ignatian Spirituality.com

Made Greater by Love

Joseph A. Tetlow, SJ

[The concept of humility] often brings to mind images of someone despised and rejected, as Jesus was in the end. It may be that God the Father would choose that for the one who asks to live as the Son lived. It certainly happens: those who proclaim the Good News are incarcerated for long years, for instance. But it is crucial to note that if someone provokes others to despise and reject him except when he is doing what must be done for Christ's sake, he cannot be thought humble. A fool, perhaps; not humble. Always the prayer must be that the Father allow you to imitate in your own time the way of Jesus of Nazareth, so long as you do not sin, and no one else sins, either.

The lover in this case is made greater by love. The Beloved chose to empty himself, taking on the ways and characteristics of a servant. He did not mind being told that he was seriously mistaken about God and the people. He did not mind being considered mad. And his way led to great suffering and death. The person who wishes to be meek and humble as Jesus was can say to the Father honestly, "Treat me as you treated your own Son."

Making Choices in Christ

Review of the Day for Managers

Paul Brian Campbell, SJ

Imagine you're at home at the end of another busy day at work. Instead of plopping down in front of the TV, you review your day at work. Some questions you might ask yourself:

- From your perspective as a manager, what was the high point of the day?

- Can you discern a pattern in what constitutes high points?

- What can you do to increase the number and duration of these high points? The low point of the day. . . . Again, look for reasons and patterns.

- What would you do differently if you were given the chance for a "do over"?

- When were you working at your best during the day? Recall as many details as you can. What made it your best work?

- When did you struggle to stay focused and engaged? Was this an isolated incident, or is this something you deal with a lot of the time?

- How hectic was the day? Do you prefer to be busy and on-the-go all the time, or would you rather have more time to pause and reflect? Why?

- Think about each of your direct reports. Imagine how he/she might have pictured interacting with you. Do you think there might be a disconnect between his/her perceptions and reality? Why?

- What concrete things could you do to improve communication between you and your direct reports?

- Look toward tomorrow.

- Are you going to make any changes in your demeanor, communication styles, and attitudes?

Ignatian Spirituality.com

AMDG

Kirk Roberts
Jesuit High School, Tampa, Florida

I am supposed to do everything in life for one reason:
    the greater glory of God.
Yet I spend most of my life unconcerned with this;
I waste it on petty things.
God, please grant me clear vision,
The vision to work for the greater glory of your name.
Please help me to wake up each morning with this
    in mind.
Help me to clear my mind of minor details that only
    distract me from my purpose.
Keep away the indifference that fogs humankind.
Point me where your people need help
So that I may go to bed each night knowing the world is
    a better place,
And your vision has been fulfilled.

In All Things

Human Ingenuity or Divine Providence? Why Not Both?

Chris Lowney

How are we to interpret the alternately serendipitous and disappointing, unexpected and unpredictable, courses of our lives? What is happening when death or financial disaster forces us to reconsider what we want from life, when teachers or mentors find and nurture talent we didn't know we had, when we succeed beyond our wildest imaginings, when managers steer our careers in fortuitous directions, when we aren't offered the job we wanted so badly, when friends point out opportunities we didn't know existed, or when we persist in pursuing a passion against all odds of success, only to find that success and fulfillment eventually come? Do such cases merely vindicate human ingenuity, resilience, and imagination? Or is God, too, at work in some ineffable way, as Hopkins says, "play[ing] in ten thousand places / Lovely in limbs, and lovely in eyes not his"?

Why not both? That's how I read Ignatius, the former military commander and take-charge, type-A personality who nonetheless attuned himself to read God's will in the subtle promptings of consolations and desolations. Or, as expressed in a great mantra of Jesuit spirituality, "Find God in all things."

Heroic Living

The Hinterland Becomes the Heartland

Margaret Silf

What if that shadowy mystery beyond the span of our years turns out to be the real country to which our earthly days are just the fragmented signposts? What if the unconscious realms in which our conscious minds are floating turn out to be the embryonic sac that is beckoning us toward a reality far beyond imagination? What if that of my life that seems so total, so final, and so absolute turns out to be the map into the hinterland of my eternal reality?

How reluctant we are to let go of the containing walls and risk a life beyond the circumscription. It seems easier to survive the slavery of Egypt than to venture into Sinai, and we convince ourselves that our slavery is freedom and our helplessness is a proud independence. The map changes radically when our walls come down and the real roads, that were always there, though impassable, are opened up. Then the hinterland becomes the heartland, where real life can really be lived.

Inner Compass

Ignatius of Loyola

A Man beyond Categories
Ronald Modras

What an Optimist!
Jim Manney

Quotes from the Spiritual Exercises
Ignatius of Loyola

Magis: A Holy Boldness

Ignatius's Two Best-Known Prayers
Ignatius of Loyola

Suscipe: The Radical Prayer
Amy Welborn

What's Next?
Jim Manney

Ten Characteristics of Ignatian Spirituality
Paul Brian Campbell, SJ

A Choice at Every Moment
Tim Muldoon

Women in His Life
*Katherine Dyckman, Mary Garvin, and
Elizabeth Liebert*

Ignatius the Theologian
Jules J. Toner, SJ

A Man beyond Categories

Ronald Modras

Ignatius Loyola has never been easy to categorize. The stereotype of an ex-soldier founding a military order to fight Protestantism is inaccurate and misleading. The metaphor of the Christian as a "soldier of Christ" was commonplace in the sixteenth century, found in the works of the scholarly Erasmus as well as those of Ignatius. Indeed, the romantic novels Ignatius read as a teenager probably had a far greater influence on his ideas about doing chivalrous deeds in God's army than did his brief exploit in battle. That's why his *Spiritual Exercises* and the spirituality that it fosters are more easily described than defined and why the genesis of his spirituality, not only the specific exercises but also its entire worldview, needs to be described in terms of his life experiences. Ignatian spirituality is profoundly biographical.

Ignatian Humanism

What an Optimist!

Jim Manney

Ignatius of Loyola was a soldier, a mystic, a writer, a teacher. He founded an order renowned for education, missionary work, learning, and devotional piety. He invented the modern practice of spiritual direction. The more you learn about him, the more complex he seems.

I like two things about Ignatius. A person formed in Ignatian spirituality is said to be a "contemplative in action." To me this means bringing prayer and work together. This is what I try to do all day. It's what my friends and colleagues try to do all day. Ignatius rightly said that this is the central challenge of life, and he had much to say about how to do it. Nothing is more relevant to life than this.

The second thing is a question that Ignatius would have us continually ask of ourselves: What do you really want? Peel away the layers of desires, fears, ambitions, and dreams and get in touch with the deepest desire of your heart. Ignatius believed that when you touch what the poet Hopkins called the "dearest freshness, deep-down things," you'll find God there.

What an optimist! That's another thing I like about Ignatius.

Ignatian Spirituality.com

Quotes from the Spiritual Exercises

Ignatius of Loyola

Permit the Creator to deal directly with the creature, and the creature directly with his Creator and Lord. [15]

Be more eager to put a good interpretation on another's statement than to condemn it as false. [22]

What have I done for Christ? What am I doing for Christ? What ought I to do for Christ? [53]

It is not much knowledge that fills and satisfies the soul, but the intimate understanding and relish of the truth. [2]

Love ought to manifest itself in deeds rather than in words. [230]

The Spiritual Exercises of St. Ignatius

Magis: A Holy Boldness

34th General Congregation of the Society of Jesus

Those who wish to give greater proof of their love, and to distinguish themselves in whatever concerns the service of the Eternal King and the Lord of all, will not only offer themselves entirely for the work . . . but make offerings of greater value and of more importance. (SE 97)

The *magis* is not simply one among others in a list of Jesuit characteristics. It permeates them all. The entire life of Ignatius was a pilgrim search for the *magis*, the ever greater glory of God, the ever fuller service of our neighbor, the more universal good, the more effective apostolic means. "Mediocrity has no place in Ignatius's worldview."

Jesuits are never content with the status quo, the known, the tried, the already existing. We are constantly driven to discover, redefine, and reach out for the magis. For us, frontiers and boundaries are not obstacles or ends, but new challenges to be faced, new opportunities to be welcomed. Indeed, ours is a holy boldness, "a certain apostolic aggressivity," typical of our way of proceeding.

"Characteristics of Our Way of Proceeding"

Ignatius's Two Best-Known Prayers

Ignatius of Loyola

Suscipe

Take, Lord, and receive all my liberty,
my memory, my understanding, and my entire will,
all that I have and possess.
You have given all to me.
To you, O Lord, I return it.
All is yours; dispose of it wholly according to your will.
Give me your love and your grace,
for this is sufficient for me.

The Spiritual Exercises

Prayer for Generosity

Eternal Word, only begotten Son of God,
Teach me true generosity.
Teach me to serve you as you deserve,
To give without counting the cost,
To fight heedless of wounds,
To labor without seeking rest,
To sacrifice myself without thought of any reward
Save the knowledge that I have done your will.
Amen.

Hearts on Fire

Suscipe: The Radical Prayer

Amy Welborn

> *Take, Lord, and receive all my liberty, my memory,*
> *my understanding, and my entire will, all that I*
> *have and possess. Thou hast given all to me. To Thee,*
> *O Lord, I return it. All is Thine, dispose of it wholly*
> *according to Thy will. Give me Thy love and Thy*
> *grace, for this is sufficient for me.*

The more you roll this prayer around in your soul . . . the more radical it is revealed to be. Ignatius offers the account of "three classes of men" who have been given a sum of money, and who all want to rid themselves of it because they know their attachment to this worldly good impedes their salvation.

The first class would really like to rid themselves of the attachment, but the hour of death comes, and they haven't even tried. The second class would also like to give up the attachment, but do so, conveniently, without actually giving anything up.

The third class wants to get rid of the *attachment* to the money, which they, like the others, know is a burden standing in the way. But they make no stipulations as to how this attachment is relinquished; they are indifferent about the method. Whatever God wants, they want. In a word, they are the free ones.

The Words We Pray, adapted

What's Next?

Jim Manney

St. Ignatius is the exemplar of the journeying Christian. Hardly anything turned out the way he thought it would when he undertook it. He thought he should live a life of penance and austerity. That was a wrong direction. He went to the Holy Land thinking he would live his life there. He was sent home. He set out on a career of lay evangelism. The church stopped him. He thought the Jesuits should live unencumbered by commitments, ready to go anywhere. They wound up running a vast network of schools.

With all these false starts, why is Ignatius regarded as the master of discernment? Because he saw that the journey is the thing. He called himself "the pilgrim." He travelled a long way, and at every step he was alert to the still small voice pointing him to what's next.

That's the thing to think about: "What's next?"

Ignatian Spirituality.com

Ten Characteristics of Ignatian Spirituality

Paul Brian Campbell, SJ

1. Union of minds and hearts—as brothers and sisters, we listen for the God who is present among us, admitting no division based on ethnicity, nationality, background, age, or gender.

2. Flexibility and adaptability—(e.g., 16th century Jesuits wearing Chinese robes and generally adapting to various cultures; respecting people's lived experience.)

3. *Ad Majorem Dei Gloriam* (For the greater glory of God)—praising God and dedicating oneself to participate in God's healing work in the world.

4. "The world is charged with the grandeur of God"—the positive, energetic, and engaged vision of God's constant interaction with creation.

5. Faith that does justice—the realization that there can be no true expression of faith where concerns for justice and human dignity are missing.

6. Inner freedom (the result of self-awareness and discernment.)

7. Contemplation in action—not a monastic existence, but an active one that is, at the same time, infused with prayer.

8. Reflection (Self-awareness/Discernment) leading to Gratitude which leads to Service (linked to becoming a "man or woman for others"—big Ignatian buzzwords.)

9. Personal relationship with Christ and love for the Church (bruised and broken as it often is.)

10. Finding God in all things

unpublished papers

A Choice at Every Moment

Tim Muldoon

At every moment of my life I have two options. If I allow it, God will form my heart more and more in the image of his Son. I can act in faith to let God lead me into an unknown place that I cannot know and cannot guarantee I will fully understand or enjoy. Like the one who is brought out of a cave into the light of the sun, I may be dazzled and disoriented by the place where God leads me. I may wish to return to my darkness, where I felt safe and at home.

God has created me for a purpose, and will at every moment of my life seek to lead me toward it. I must do my best to remove the obstacles to his gentle urging, reaching out in faith in imitation of Jesus. I may reach a moment of crisis, as Jesus did, a moment of sheer terror in trusting God. I may find myself on the path of suffering, like Jesus. Jesus shows me that nothing that life throws at me can compare with what God wants to bring forth from my life. He will bring to fruition what he has started. He has clothed me in beauty and goodness, capable of deep and lasting love, and I will delight in it if I but allow him to form me.

Ignatian Spirituality.com

Women in His Life

Katherine Dyckman, Mary Garvin, and Elizabeth Liebert

Women sensitive to the ways of God appeared regularly in Ignatius's life after his conversion. Particularly prominent are the women of Manresa. . . . Testimonies for Ignatius's canonization process actually reveal more about the ladies of Manresa than his *Autobiography*. Known for their laudable lives of prayer and service to the poor even before they met Ignatius, they welcomed him as he shared with them the fruit of his own spiritual experience. The chroniclers describe them as "very honorable women, good Christians, virtuous, and of good reputation." One of the most influential was Inéz Pascual who, with her friend Jerònima Calver, initially met a limping Ignatius on the way from Montserrat to Manresa. They first directed him to the hospice Jerònima ran and continued to provide him with food and shelter as needed. Later, Ignatius stayed at the homes of these and other women.

The Spiritual Exercises Reclaimed

Ignatius the Theologian

Jules J. Toner, SJ

Ignatius was a theologian, even a great one, in the sense of having through mystical experience an experiential knowledge of God and of the Christian mysteries. In the realm of teachable truth, Ignatius was also a great theologian, but not a speculative one. His theology is purely practical; it revolves around how to find and respond to God in all things and, especially, how to find God's will and do it for the glory of God. His theology of seeking and finding God's will is found embedded in his immediately practical instructions and counsels on how to prepare for and go about discerning it and in his descriptions of his own efforts to do so.

Discerning God's Will

Relationships

What Intimacy Requires
Margaret Silf

As Kingfishers Catch Fire
Gerard Manley Hopkins, SJ

What to Do about Intrigues and Lies
Ignatius of Loyola

Telling Our Story
James Martin, SJ

The Right Presupposition

Ignatius of Loyola

For a good relationship to develop . . . a mutual respect is very necessary. This may be especially true in areas of scriptural and theological presentation. Every good Christian adopts a more positive acceptance of someone's statement rather than a rejection of it out of hand. And so a favorable interpretation . . . should always be given to the other's statement, and confusions should be cleared up with Christian understanding. So, too, if actual error seems to be held, an attempt at a better interpretation should be made so that a more correct understanding may develop.

Draw Me Into Your Friendship

The Great Gift of Relationships

Joseph A. Tetlow, SJ

The Examen of relationships asks that you grow conscious of a reality we take so much for granted that we do not think about it at all. How often do you note that the sun rose this morning? How much do you value the water that comes from your tap? We treat our relationships rather like that. They are just *there*. They do not take thinking about except perhaps in special circumstances like an argument or a celebration. But each relationship is a gift greater than today's sun, and each person given to you to love and be loved by is as indispensable as the pure water you thoughtlessly drink.

"Examen: Persons in Relationship"

Gratitude Leads to Forgiveness

Lyn Holley Doucet

To St. Ignatius, everything was a gift. This humble saint never felt that he deserved anything. In fact, he was sometimes amazed that God was good to him at all. He was touched that God did not want to punish the world but wanted to shower humanity with good gifts. In his worldview, all came from God and all returned to God. Ignatius gave himself completely to God's will, in which he found the higher gifts, the things that did not decay or fade away. . . . Ignatius leads us to love as God loves, without condition. Despite persecution Ignatius forgave others.

It is easy to become bitter when others hurt us or when our dreams are crushed. This is a very human response, and these feelings come to most of us. But . . . we can allow our hearts to be touched by the beauty of the world and all of God's goodness. We can humbly begin to forgive others and experience healing as we realize that all is a gift.

A Healing Walk with St. Ignatius

Go in His Door

Ignatius of Loyola

Whenever we wish to win someone over and engage him in the greater service of God our Lord, we should use the same strategy for good which the enemy employs to draw a good soul to evil. He enters through the other's door and comes out his own. He enters with the other by not opposing his ways but by praising them. He acts familiarly with the soul, suggesting good and holy thoughts which bring peace to the good soul. Later he tries, little by little, to come out his own door, always suggesting some error or illusion under the appearance of good, but which will always be evil. So we with a good purpose can praise or agree with another concerning some particular good thing, dissembling whatever else may be wrong. After thus gaining his confidence, we shall have better success. In this sense we go in with him his way but come out our own.

We should ingratiate ourselves with those who are sad or tempted, speak at length and show great satisfaction and cheerfulness, both interior and exterior, so as to draw them to the opposite of what they feel, for their greater edification and consolation.

Letters of Saint Ignatius of Loyola

When in Conflict

Paul Coutinho, SJ

St. Ignatius offers a model for assertive behavior in The Spiritual Exercises. The first step is to find a good interpretation for what the other person is saying or doing. It might be good to see the hurtful behavior as coming from either ignorance or unconscious pain. If I believe that the behavior is more deliberate, then St. Ignatius encourages me to seek clarity with the other person. I can ask the person what he really means by what he is saying or doing or I can tell him how I feel when he says or does something that seems hurtful, or I can tell him what I would like from him.

If that does not seem to work, then the third step is to correct the person's behavior with kindness and love—to use every appropriate means to help the other person while doing something constructive with his or her negative behavior. . . . Sometimes this love will motivate the person to change his or her behavior. But I know that not everyone will change; this is why the root belief that people must be fair and kind to me is so dangerous. This is where freedom comes in; even if the person doesn't change, I remain a free and loving person—not an angry, resentful one—by responding assertively.

How Big Is Your God? adapted

The Trouble Lies Within

Ignatius of Loyola

Ignatius, writing to a troubled Jesuit:

You are mistaken in thinking that the cause of your disquiet, or little progress in the Lord, is due so much to the place, or your superiors, or your brethren. This disquiet comes from within and not from without. I mean from your lack of humility, obedience, and prayer, your slight mortification, in a word your little fervor in advancing in the way of perfection.

You might change residence, superiors, and brethren, but if you do not change the interior man, you will never do good. And you will everywhere be the same, unless you succeed in being humble, obedient, devout, and mortified in your self-love. This is the only change you should seek. I mean that you should try to change the interior man and lead him back like a servant to God.

Letters of Saint Ignatius of Loyola

Facing Death Fearlessly

Lyn Holley Doucet

Ignatius was anointed for death several times in his life. Toward the end of his life he forbade himself to think about death, as the idea of it gave him such consolation. Isn't this the model for all of us Christians—that we face death fearlessly?

As we grow in faith and become more mature on our journey, we can turn our eyes to the final end. For surely, we all must die. The only question is, what will our death be like? Will we go peacefully, having given peace to those around us? Can we look forward to seeing God face to face? Or will we still be clinging to this life and to our cares, vices, and pettiness? Well, even if we are, we can know that God is ever willing to forgive us, to welcome us home again.

A Healing Walk with St. Ignatius

It's All about Intimacy

William A. Barry, SJ

Prayer is a matter of relationship. Intimacy is the basic issue, not answers to problems or resolutions "to be better." Many of life's problems and challenges have no answers; we can only live with and through them. Problems and challenges, however, can be faced and lived through with more peace and resilience if people know that they are not alone. A man's wife will not return from the dead, but the pain is more bearable when he has poured out his sorrow, his anger, and his despair to God and has experienced God's intimate presence.

Letting God Come Close

What Intimacy Requires

Margaret Silf

Intimacy, whether with God or with another human being, challenges us to come closer, to take risks, to be open to change and transformation in a dynamic relationship that we cannot control. It engages us in:

- *listening*—by opening our hearts to God. We learn to become inwardly still and receptive to what God wants to show us,

- *disclosing*—revealing ourselves to God in prayer, just as we are,

- *sharing*—allowing the life of the Lord to become deeply connected to our own by absorbing his Word and by sharing in the events of his living, his dying, and his rising,

- *reflecting*—deepening our experience of God by becoming more and more aware of the ways in which he meets us in our daily lives,

- *giving*—freely offering to others the gifts we have received ourselves; sharing God's love and spreading his Kingdom.

Inner Compass

As Kingfishers Catch Fire

Gerard Manley Hopkins, SJ

As kingfishers catch fire, dragonflies draw flame;
As tumbled over rim in roundy wells
Stones ring; like each tucked string tells, each hung bell's
Bow swung finds tongue to fling out broad its name;
Each mortal thing does one thing and the same:
Deals out that being indoors each one dwells;
Selves—goes itself; myself it speaks and spells,
Crying *What I do is me: for that I came.*

I say more: the just man justices;
Keeps grace: that keeps all his goings graces;
Acts in God's eye what in God's eye he is—
Christ—for Christ plays in ten thousand places
Lovely in limbs, and lovely in eyes not his
To the Father through the features of men's faces.

Poems of Gerard Manley Hopkins

What to Do about Intrigues and Lies

Ignatius of Loyola

You speak of the enmities, the intrigues, and untruths which have been circulated about you. I am not at all surprised at this, not even if it were worse than it is. For just as soon as you determined to bend every effort to procure the praise, honor, and service of God our Lord, you declared war against the world. . . .

If we wish absolutely to live in honor and to be held in esteem by our neighbors, we can never be solidly rooted in God our Lord, and it will be impossible for us to remain unscathed when we meet their affronts. . . .

I would rather fix my attention on one fault that I had committed than on all the evil that might be said of me.

Letters of Saint Ignatius of Loyola

Telling Our Story

James Martin, SJ

Each night at the Public Theater, the cast of *Judas* told, to a new audience, the tale of Jesus of Nazareth and his circle of friends. Watching the actors reminded me of the original tellers of the tale, who were also the original participants in the drama: people such as Peter and Mary Magdalene and Matthew and Thomas and Simon the Zealot. After witnessing Jesus' life over a three-year period—seeing his amazing miracles and hearing his parables and stories and being witnesses to his passion, death, and resurrection—the first disciples would have found it impossible to be silent, to refrain from telling their own versions of the tale. They, like many people in the arts, would have been compelled to express what they had witnessed.

A Jesuit Off-Broadway

The Spiritual Exercises

Three Causes of Desolation
Mark E. Thibodeaux, SJ

Ignatius's Mission: Help People Experience
God's Presence
Ronald Modras

What People Say Doesn't Matter
Paul Coutinho, SJ

The Purpose of Human Life

Joseph A. Tetlow, SJ

Paraphrasing from the Spiritual Exercises:

Every person in the world is so put together that by praising, revering, and living according to the will of God our Lord he or she will safely reach the Reign of God. This is the original purpose of each human life. Every other thing on the face of the earth is meant for humankind, to help each person come to the original purpose God has put in each of us.

The only thing that makes sense in the use of all other things, then, is that a person uses everything that helps realize that original purpose deep in the self, and turns away from everything that alienates us from the original purpose in ourselves.

Choosing Christ in the World

A Lesson from a Homeless Man

Bill Creed, SJ

Only when I began to give the Spiritual Exercises to homeless men did I learn how inextricably linked are disordered affections and ordered relationships. One very intelligent, well-educated, thirty-year old man, on the streets for several years, addicted to cocaine, alcohol, and sex, sought me out as he attempted to find sobriety. His repeated failures at becoming sober without explicitly asking God for help finally led him to a spiritual path. He learned that he did not have the strength to sustain sobriety without daily reliance on God. He learned that he could not stay with the recovery process in a twelve-step program without daily prayer, without claiming his own goodness and purpose.

Eventually, after several years of sobriety and practicing the twelve steps, and after growth in prayer through spiritual direction, he did the Nineteenth Annotation full Exercises. This helped him identify how embedded were the attitudes that had led him to addictive behavior on the streets. The Exercises opened him to the mystery of how deeply God loves him and wants him to join Christ in serving others. As he became freed from the external and internal disordered attitudes and behaviors, he was able, not only to retain employment, but was also sought out for advancement. He was also able to sustain and commit to authentic relationship. His choices became more congruent with his purpose in life.

unpublished papers

The Central Question: Who Am I?

George A. Aschenbrenner, SJ

"Who am I?" is the central question for us all. Some people are haunted by it, while others have not yet acknowledged its rumbling in their subconscious. Yet it is always there. A great variety of answers bombard you from parents, friends, enemies, chance acquaintances, and many other people. Our secular culture has its own pervasive answer, sometimes as blatant as a billboard, a television advertisement, a slick frothy newsmagazine but usually more subtle, like mist on a damp, overcast day. The result, however, is the same: a clammy dampness that does not cleanse but contaminates.

Where does one turn for self-discovery? The answer to that question can be significant in itself. In the Exercises we turn to God's revelation in a profoundly personal experience of mutual self-revelation with God in Jesus.

Stretched for Greater Glory

Intimate Understanding

Ignatius of Loyola

The one who explains to another the method and order of meditating or contemplating should narrate accurately the facts of the contemplation or meditation. Let him adhere to the points, and add only a short or summary explanation. The reason for this is that when one in meditating takes the solid foundation of facts, and goes over it and reflects on it for himself, he may find something that makes them a little clearer or better understood. This may arise either from his own reasoning, or from the grace of God enlightening his mind. Now this produces greater spiritual relish and fruit than if one in giving the Exercises had explained and developed the meaning at great length. For it is not much knowledge that fills and satisfies the soul, but the intimate understanding and relish of the truth.

The Spiritual Exercises

Holistic Exercises

Katherine Dyckman, Mary Garvin, and Elizabeth Liebert

Although many commonly assume that the Spiritual Exercises are highly rational and "left brain," they actually evoke a far more holistic range of competencies. "Ignatian contemplation" involves rich use of the imagination, and a wide range of affects plays a crucial part in the experience of the Exercises. Memory undergirds the examen, a prayer form Ignatius thought so significant in the development of a continually discerning spirit that he never speaks of omitting it in favor of a greater good. Data gleaned through the senses grounds the repetitions Ignatius encourages, simplifying, focusing and embodying material generated in meditations and contemplations. Repeated prayers, formal and spontaneous vocal prayer, spiritual reading and reflections on the essentials of the Christian faith all find their place on the palette of spiritual exercises. Any and all may be used, their selection and timing based upon the needs of the individual. Ignatius states his goal explicitly: that persons "may become better able to profit from the exercises and to find their prayer a pleasing experience." Insisting on a single prayer style for all is definitely not Ignatian.

The Spiritual Exercises Reclaimed

The Present Moment Is the Only Real Moment

Bill Creed, SJ

The spiritual life always concerns itself with the present. Retreatants are very inclined to worry about the future and be guilty about the past. It is important to set goals for the future and to implement ways to achieve those goals. It is also important to review the past, claim the history of grace and sin and more grace. But the Present Moment is the only real moment. . . . Directors of the Exercises are always inviting retreatants to live in the now moment, because the present is the only moment of grace.

unpublished papers

The Enemy Likes to Stay Hidden

Ignatius of Loyola

In his rules for discernment of spirits, Ignatius discusses the strategy of the evil spirit.

Our enemy may also be compared in his manner of acting to a false lover. He seeks to remain hidden and does not want to be discovered. If such a lover speaks with evil intention to the daughter of a good father, or to the wife of a good husband, and seeks to seduce them, he wants his words and solicitations kept secret. . . . In the same way when the enemy of our human nature tempts a just soul with his wiles and seductions, he earnestly desires that they be received secretly and kept secret. But if one manifests them to a confessor, or to some other spiritual person who understands his deceits and malicious designs, the evil one is very much vexed. For he knows that he cannot succeed in his evil undertaking, once his evident deceits have been revealed.

The Spiritual Exercises

Three Ways to Collude with the World

Joseph A. Tetlow, SJ

First, there is benign secularism. . . . We join civic movements and help the needy because that's what our neighbors do. We are good to our families and honest in the workplace. There is no immediate harm in this way, but neither is there anything more than a secular spirit, even though people today call it spirituality.

The second form of collusion, seen particularly in the affluent first world, is the search for pleasure. . . . Those who follow this way are the target of advertising. . . . Their less lovely side manifests self-indulgence, lust, envy—all seen as acceptable social mores. . . .

Finally, there is the collusion of succumbing to darkness. . . . But most of the works of the dark are not manifest. Hatred, vengeance, violence, self-destructive habits—these flourish in the dark corners of the sinful human self.

In your heart of hearts, you may loathe the dark and leap to the light. But in everyday life, you will find yourself in the twilight of benign secularism. . . . You will find safety in Christ's standard only if you resolutely begin everything with thanks to God and keep watching what you are doing and why you are doing it.

Making Choices in Christ

Three Causes of Desolation

Mark E. Thibodeaux, SJ

1. I have fallen into sin and God has allowed desolation to come as a natural consequence.

2. God allows desolation to come in order to "test me." He knows that some gifts and graces come only through struggle on my part. Much like a teacher who tests even her gifted students in order that they grow stronger in the field, so does God allow desolation to challenge and stretch me.

3. God allows desolation to come in order to give me the great gift of humility, which is a core virtue for Ignatius and of which Ignatius says one could never have enough. If my spiritual life were filled with nothing but consolation, I could well become spiritually prideful. I could begin to think that I am the source of the graces that come from God. God allows desolation to remind me that "all is the gift and grace of God our Lord" and that I can do nothing without him.

God's Voice Within

Ignatius's Mission: Help People Experience God's Presence

Ronald Modras

Iñigo became convinced that experiencing God in a direct and immediate way was not a special favor reserved for a few select mystics. If God was willing to speak directly to a sinner like him, God would speak to anyone—anyone, at least, who was willing to take the time to be still, listen, and pray. If people were willing to spend an extended period of time in solitude and prayer, daydreaming about Jesus the way he had at Loyola and Manresa, then he, Iñigo, could help them experience God and learn God's will for them. This, he became convinced, was his mission from God: to help people experience God's presence and learn God's will by directing them in making the Spiritual Exercises.

Ignatian Humanism

What People Say Doesn't Matter

Paul Coutinho, SJ

Jesus shows us that what people say does not matter. The people who shout, "Hosanna!" today will be the very same people who shout, "Crucify him!" tomorrow. The only thing that matters is what God says to me and what God feels toward me: I am pleased with you, my favor rests on you, my delight is in you. What matters is not if people say good or bad things about me; what matters is the way I feel in my relationship with God and that I am free. As with the pleasures of life, the good opinion of people is a good thing; to be considered honorable, moral, just, and kind is a good thing. But I cannot build my happiness around, or find meaning for my life in, what people say and think about me.

How Big Is Your God?

Desires, Discernment, and Decision Making

His Eyes Were Opened a Little
Ignatius of Loyola

Keeping Things Secret
Mark E. Thibodeaux, SJ

Interplay between Experience,
Reflection, Decision and Action
34th General Congregation of the Society of Jesus

A Prayer for Discernment
Pedro Arrupe, SJ

A Process for Group Decision Making
William Byron, SJ

The Real Enemy Is Satan
William A. Barry, SJ

True Desire Is Fire in the Heart

George A. Aschenbrenner, SJ

A constant refrain running through the whole of the *Exercises* is the invitation to pray for what you desire. The whole experience happens on the level of desire of the heart. Ignatius believes that desire, as the deepest, most personal experience of grace, always reveals a person's true identity and is the birthplace of commitment. . . . What is deeply desired is the grace in each exercise from beginning to end.

Praying for what one deeply desires is never easy. It pushes us into a place where a serious conflict is raging for us all, a conflict sometimes not acknowledged but always crucial to our true identity. To discover what we deeply, truly desire forces us to wade into a swamp of needs, expectations, demands, casual wishes, moods, obligations, and much more. Your deepest, truest desire may coincide with one or another of these interior experiences but will always cut deeper into your heart than any of them. True desire is fire in the heart. But, rather than simply dancing on the tips of the flashing flames, it quietly burns deep in the white-hot coals. These deepest, truest desires constitute and reveal a person's core identity.

Stretched for Greater Glory

[margin handwritten note: desire is The deepest, most personal experience of grace.]

God Needs to Hear Our Desires

William A. Barry, SJ

Often we tell ourselves, or we are told, in an effort to quell our desires, to look at the good we already have. We can feel guilty and ungrateful for desiring what we want. But if we suppress our desires without being satisfied that God has heard us, then we pull back from honesty with God. Often, the result for our relationship with God is polite distance or cool civility. Perhaps God cannot or will not grant what we want, but for the sake of the continued development of the relationship we need to keep letting God know our real desires until we are satisfied or have heard or felt some response. . . .

A woman may, for example, be experiencing a "dark night of the soul" and not like it at all. She may desire that it be removed. She may be helped by the knowledge that others before her have experienced the same thing and have been the better for it, but such knowledge does not have to satisfy her desire to be rid of the dark night. A short circuit in the relationship might occur if she tells herself or is told by her spiritual director to squelch her desire "because the experience is good for you." What she needs to experience is God's response, not a theorem of spiritual theology.

Letting God Come Close

What Do I Really Want?

J. Michael Sparough, SJ; Jim Manney; Tim Hipskind, SJ

The question to be constantly asked in decision making is, *What do I really want?* Deep down, that's what God wants, too. God wants what is best for us. This isn't something repugnant or burdensome or sad or difficult. The way of life that God desires for us is the way of life we desire. *What do I really want?* is a simple question. But simple isn't the same as easy. Usually this question is quite difficult to answer. Our deepest desires are obscured by pride, fears, ambitions, and attachments to money, honor, security, and a host of other things. The process of discernment is essentially a process of stripping away these false desires and finding the desires at the core of our selves. Discernment of spirits is a way of grasping what these deep desires are.

What's Your Decision?

The True Spirit in My Life

Mark E. Thibodeaux, SJ

Begin to reflect on a time when you were clearly in a period of consolation—a time of deep inner peace, during which you experienced great desires of faith, hope, and love. It might be a time of exterior sadness or tragedy but of interior peace and tranquility. Ask God to reveal this time to you so that you can learn from it. Go back to that place of deep inner peace. Here are a few ways you might reflect on moments of consolation.

Read and ponder Jesus' words in John 14:27. What is the peace of Christ like? How do you experience it? How is it not the peace that the world gives? Note how this peace does not imply that all interior and exterior problems are solved and resolved but that you have a new and different relationship with those problems.

Looking back on that period of consolation, ponder how close you felt to God then and how natural it seemed to move toward greater faith, hope, and love.

Looking back on that period of consolation, remember how easy it was to recognize "God laboring through all created things and events," as St. Ignatius put it. See how clear it was for you to see God's hand in every aspect of life, even the difficult ones.

God's Voice Within

Ignatius's Big Discovery

J. Michael Sparough, SJ; Jim Manney; Tim Hipskind, SJ

The point has often been made that the Christian gospel is a story of strength and triumph arising from weakness and defeat. The Savior is a poor man in a provincial, backwater land. Salvation comes about through suffering and death. In the words of Mary's Magnificat prayer: "He has brought down the powerful from their thrones, and lifted up the lowly; he has filled the hungry with good things, and sent the rich away empty."

We're afflicted with divided hearts that cause us to be burdened by angst, uncertainty, and fear when making important decisions. But this very confusion of thoughts and feelings is the place where we find God's footprints. It's the raw material for discernment.

This was Ignatius's great discovery.

What's Your Decision?

Discernment Is Practical and Personal

J. Michael Sparough, SJ; Jim Manney; Tim Hipskind, SJ

Here's a working definition: *discernment of God's will is the act of distinguishing between options while consciously calling on God for assistance.* It's *practical*—it involves the concrete circumstances of daily life. Discernment is about a choice that needs to be made between options that are real possibilities. It's not about vague longings or nebulous dreams.

Our definition presumes that we'll get an answer. *God touches us personally.* God doesn't talk in broad generalities or lay down rules that everyone has to conform to. Again, discernment is practical and personalized.

When we say that discernment involves "consciously calling on God for assistance," we mean that the process of discernment is essentially a dynamic one. It involves a relationship with God, with the world around us, with the people around us, and ultimately with ourselves. The rhythm of this relationship is call-and-response; God invites, we answer. Decision making can be compared to the back-and-forth call-and-response music of a gospel choir.

The price of admission to this gospel concert is a desire to choose the best of a number of good options. That's the one necessary thing.

What's Your Decision?

His Eyes Were Opened a Little

Ignatius of Loyola

Ignatius's account of his first insights into discernment.

This succession of diverse thoughts was of long duration, and they were either of worldly achievements which he desired to accomplish, or those of God which took hold of his imagination to such an extent, that worn out with the struggle, he turned them all aside and gave his attention to other things.

There was, however, this difference. When he was thinking of the things of the world he was filled with delight, but afterwards he was dry and dissatisfied. And when he thought of going barefoot to Jerusalem and of eating nothing but herbs and performing the other rigors he saw that the saints had performed, he was consoled, not only when he entertained these thoughts, but even after dismissing them he remained cheerful and satisfied. But he paid no attention to this, nor did he stop to weigh the difference until one day his eyes were opened a little and he began to wonder at the difference and to reflect on it, learning from experience that one kind of thoughts left him sad and the other cheerful. Thus, step by step, he came to recognize the difference between the two spirits that moved him, the one being from the evil spirit, the other from God.

St. Ignatius' Own Story

Keeping Things Secret

Mark E. Thibodeaux, SJ

Ignatius warns against the false spirit's trick of getting me to keep things secret from my mentors and companions. Common sense requires that I not tell everyone everything all the time. However . . . if I find myself keeping secrets, chances are, the false spirit is afoot. When I am in desolation, I cannot trust my own judgment; I will need the objectivity and sensibility of the wise and loving people around me. Otherwise, I will be lost in my private fog and will not even be aware of the fog's existence. The spirit of desolation will attempt to leave me in this fog by keeping me from those who are standing outside it. I will convince myself that:

- He wouldn't understand.

- She'll overreact.

- We don't have time to talk about it now.

- It's not that important anyhow.

- It's too embarrassing to mention.

- He'll be ashamed of me. It will disappoint him.

- I need to work this out before I tell her about it.

- I'll deal with it later—it can wait.

- It will resolve itself.

- He's too busy to be bothered with this.
- She's dealing with her own personal issues right now.
- I know what she'll say.
- He'll be hurt . . . angry . . . disappointed.
- She's too old fashioned . . . liberal . . . judgmental to understand.

God's Voice Within

Interplay between Experience, Reflection, Decision and Action

34th General Congregation of the Society of Jesus

For a Jesuit, therefore, not just any response to the needs of the men and women of today will do. The initiative must come from the Lord laboring in events and people here and now. God invites us to join with him in his labors, on his terms, and in his way. To discover and join the Lord, laboring to bring everything to its fullness, is central to the Jesuit way of proceeding. It is the Ignatian method of prayerful discernment, which can be described as "a constant interplay between experience, reflection, decision and action, in line with the Jesuit ideal of being 'contemplatives in action.'"

"Characteristics of Our Way of Proceeding"

A Prayer for Discernment

Pedro Arrupe, SJ

Grant me, O Lord, to see everything now with new eyes,
to discern and test the spirits
that help me read the signs of the times,
to relish the things that are yours, and to communicate
     them to others.
Give me the clarity of understanding that you gave
     Ignatius.

Hearts on Fire

A Process for Group Decision Making

William Byron, SJ

- Look at your charter, mission statement, papers of incorporation, brand name, motto, or slogan. Is there room for the admission that your organization, like your nation, operates "under God"? If so, reaffirm that fact and determine not to hide it at the policy-making table.

- Have a little quiet time before and during decision-making meetings. In many cases it would be a good idea for top management or group leaders to take a few days off for a communications workshop or a management retreat to dissolve interpersonal tensions, reduce anxiety levels. . . .

- Allow for full participation in the preparation of the agenda, with provision for strong advocacy of a position early in the meeting process.

- Provide opportunities for all elements of unease to surface, followed by a quiet time when each participant can reflect on the possible sources of his or her own unease.

- Segment the meeting into time "pro" and time "con" with respect to every major issue. In each of these segments, all participants must speak, if only to agree with a point already made.

- Whoever chairs the process then tries to "read a consensus" and tests it against the group. If there is no clear consensus, the chair can probe for areas of consensus. At this juncture, some open debate may be useful. As a last resort, the group can decide by vote.

Jesuit Saturdays

The Real Enemy Is Satan

William A. Barry, SJ

The discernment of the spirits rests on the belief that the human heart is a battleground where God and the evil one struggle for mastery. Jesus of Nazareth himself believed this. In the desert he had been tempted by the evil one masquerading as an angel of light. If these were real temptations, then he, like us, had to discern the movements inspired by God from those inspired by the evil one. He, too, had to make an act of faith in who God really is, based on his experiences and his knowledge of the Scriptures of his people. Jesus came to recognize who the real enemy of God's rule is. He cast out demons and equated his power over the demons as a sign of God's coming to rule: "But if it is by the finger of God that I cast out demons, then the kingdom of God has come upon you." The majority party of the Pharisees and most Jews of the time saw the real enemy of Israel, and therefore of God, as the pagans, and especially the Roman occupiers. Over and over again Jesus warned his hearers that the real enemy was Satan.

Spirit, Style, Story

Freedom

Beware of False Humility
Ignatius of Loyola

Teach Me Your Ways
Pedro Arrupe, SJ

Patient Trust
Pierre Teilhard de Chardin, SJ

Free Indeed!
Joseph A. Tetlow, SJ

What Jesus Promised

Paul Coutinho, SJ

The Good News is that Jesus came to give us freedom—not freedom from suffering, sickness, and death, but freedom that we experience *in* suffering, *in* sickness, and *in* the face of death. Jesus never promised to get rid of suffering. He never promised to get rid of sickness. He never promised to get rid of death and dying. Jesus promised to give us the peace that the world cannot give. Jesus promised to give us the inner freedom, joy, and happiness that no one and nothing can take away from us, even in the midst of tremendous pain, suffering, sickness, and death. That is the Good News of Jesus, and that is what we see in the cross.

How Big Is Your God?

Disordered Attachments

Vinita Hampton Wright

Fear is a great indicator of disordered attachment because it focuses upon what we don't want to lose or give up. When are you afraid? What situations trigger your fear? What kinds of loss or change are most threatening to you? Spend time imagining potential situations that would threaten your attachments.

Please remember that attachments are often simply love out of balance. It's wonderful to enjoy a good meal with friends—but must you always go to an expensive restaurant or spend days cooking to provide the perfect feast? It's good that you are a loyal friend, but does that loyalty lead you to expect total devotion in return? Getting unattached means holding life lightly and with tempered expectations.

Think of the things you love and determine where some of those loves may be out of balance. Invite the Trinity to sit with you while you imagine attachments falling away. There's Jesus, who had to learn detachment when he lived a human life. There's God your parent-creator, who knows exactly how you are put together and what is utterly best for the whole of your life. There's the Holy Spirit, who longs for your soul to be at peace and for you to enjoy complete freedom to live well. Listen to what God-in-three-persons says to you.

Days of Deepening Friendship

"That's *Insane*"

James Martin, SJ

The Exercises invite us to embrace a radical freedom: "On our part," Ignatius writes, "we want not health rather than sickness, riches rather than poverty, long rather than short life, and so in all the rest; desiring and choosing only that which is most conducive for us to the end for which we are created."

One young woman, after hearing those lines, said to me, "I'm not supposed to prefer health over sickness? That's *insane*."

Of course no one wants to be sick. But in Ignatius's worldview, health should not be something clung to so tightly that the fear of illness prevents you from following God. As in "Well, I'm not going to visit my friend in the hospital, because I might get sick." Ignatius would say that in that case you may not be "indifferent" enough; health has become a sort of god, preventing you from doing good. The goal is not choosing sickness for its own sake, but moving toward the freedom of knowing that the highest good is not your own physical well-being. For most of us, this kind of complete freedom will remain a lifetime goal.

My Life with the Saints

What Indifference Really Means

Chris Lowney

Understanding personal attachments means overturning personal rocks to see what crawls out. Attachment to money is usually salve for some other debilitating ego-itch: I'm terrified of failing; I need to feel important and be the center of attention; I'm insecure about my real talent and worth.

This is what Loyola was *really* after: the internal fears, drives, and attachments that can control decisions and actions. Imagine the chief executive who undertakes an ill-advised merger because his ego inflates along with his company's balance sheet—or who backs away from a brilliant merger because he and his counterpart cannot carve out roles commensurate with their enormous egos. Imagine the sixteenth-century Jesuit reluctant to go to China, clinging to the security blanket of working on home turf surrounded by friends—or the twenty-first-century professional forgoing a wonderful career opportunity for similar reasons. Consider the controlling micromanager unable to relinquish authority to subordinates—or the person mired in a destructive relationship out of fear of being alone. All are driven by their attachments just as addicts are driven by alcohol, sex, or drugs.

These people aren't indifferent. They are not freely making choices; their inordinate attachments are in control. As a result, they don't in the end choose what will best serve them, their companies, their coworkers, or their families.

Heroic Leadership

Ignatian Indifference Is Filled with Passion

Mark E. Thibodeaux, SJ

Ignatian spirituality calls this gift of grateful availability Ignatian indifference. Obviously, this is quite different from what is normally referred to as indifference—that is, the negative attitude of not caring about something. On the contrary, Ignatian indifference is filled with passion—passion for the will of God and the good of all. If I am indifferent in this Ignatian sense, then I care so much about serving God in a quite definite way that I am willing and ready to take on anything—or give up anything—for the cause. Ignatian indifference does not ignore desires but rather taps into our deepest desire—our desire to praise, reverence, and serve God.

Why is indifference so important to discernment? If I set out to make a decision without indifference, then I'll unconsciously be steering my discernment toward the option that I want. Why discern at all if I'm not actually open to more than one possibility? But to be indifferent, I am even more than open to other possibilities—I truly *desire* to follow *any* of the perceived paths so long as it leads to God's greater glory.

God's Voice Within

Prayer to St. Francis Xavier

Luke Rothan
St. Xavier High School, Cincinnati, Ohio

Help me become a hero—
One who executes both spiritual and physical feats;
One who gives himself up to be a part of something
    greater;
One who departs on a journey and returns changed.
Help me to emphasize the *magis*—
One who does his best in every area;
One who strives to be great in all aspects of his life.
Help me become a person with and for others—
One who respects himself as well as others;
One who performs deeds not for himself, but for others.
Help me become a leader—
One who persuades others to do the right thing;
One who guides others through action, not talk.
Amen.

In All Things

Sources of Freedom

Gerald M. Fagin, SJ

We have seen two sources of freedom. The first is our experience of God's unconditional love. Knowing God's love frees us to act out of love and our deepest desires, not out of fear or a sense of inadequacy.

The second source is our trust in a God who is a faithful giver. . . . God will continue to give us what we need. Recall the parable in Luke 12:16–21: there is no need to fill our barns for the future. Jesus reminded us of the lilies of the field and the birds of the air that God cares for. We need not be anxious because God will care for us as well.

But at the deepest level, freedom flows from our passion for God alone. We are moved by God's love to center our hearts only on God. This is the heart of Ignatian indifference that sets our hearts free for love and service. In the end, this is putting on the heart of Christ, a heart that trusts in God, a heart so filled with love that it desires to let go and share, and a heart free to seek God's kingdom above all else.

Putting on the Heart of Christ

The Attitude You Should Have

William J. O'Malley, SJ

As a preface to his declaration about the Incarnation in Philippians, St. Paul said, "The attitude you should have is the one that Christ Jesus had."

Wisdom is making peace with the unchangeable. We have the freedom to face the unavoidable with dignity, to understand the transformational value that attitude works on suffering. Viktor Frankl wrote that in concentration camps, "what alone remains is 'the last of human freedoms'—the ability to choose one's attitude in a given set of circumstances." What Frankl asked is not optimism in the face of pessimism but hope in the face of hopelessness.

Are we responsible for our unmerited suffering? The answer is no. And yes. We are not responsible for our predicament as its cause—whether it be cancer or job loss or the death of a child or spouse. But we are responsible for what we do with the effects, for what we build from the rubble that fate has made of our lives.

God: The Oldest Question

Beware of False Humility

Ignatius of Loyola

Ignatius warned his friend, Sister Teresa Rejadella, that the devil would try to tempt her to keep silent about God's special graces to her.

When he sees someone so good and humble . . . [the devil] is ready with the suggestion that, should the Lord's servant happen to speak of the graces our Lord has bestowed upon him in actual deeds or merely in resolve or desire, he sins by another kind of vanity in speaking favorably of himself. In this way he tries to prevent him from speaking of any of the blessings he has received. His purpose is to prevent him from producing fruit in others as well as in himself. For he knows that, when such a person recalls to mind what he has received, he is always helped in regard to greater things. One ought, however, to be very reserved, and speak only with the motive of helping others or himself: others if he sees that they are in the proper dispositions and likely to believe him and draw some profit from what he says. Thus, when the enemy of our salvation sees that we are humble, he tries to draw us on to a humility that is excessive and counterfeit.

Letters of Saint Ignatius of Loyola

Teach Me Your Ways

Pedro Arrupe, SJ

Teach me your way of looking at people:
as you glanced at Peter after his denial,
as you penetrated the heart of the rich young man
and the hearts of your disciples.
I would like to meet you as you really are,
since your image changes those with whom you
come into contact.
Remember John the Baptist's first meeting with you?
And the centurion's feeling of unworthiness?
And the amazement of all those who saw miracles
and other wonders?
How you impressed your disciples,
the rabble in the Garden of Olives,
Pilate and his wife
and the centurion at the foot of the cross. . . .
I would like to hear and be impressed
by your manner of speaking,
listening, for example, to your discourse in the
synagogue in Capharnaum
or the Sermon on the Mount where your audience
felt you "taught as one who has authority."

The Spiritual Legacy of Pedro Arrupe

Patient Trust

Pierre Teilhard de Chardin, SJ

Above all, <u>trust in the slow work of God.</u>
We are quite naturally impatient in everything
to reach the end without delay.
We should like to skip the intermediate stages.
We are impatient of being on the way to something
unknown, something new.
And yet it is the law of all progress
that it is made by passing through
some stages of instability—
and that it may take a very long time.
And so I think it is with you;
your ideas mature gradually—let them grow,
let them shape themselves, without undue haste.
Don't try to force them on,
as though you could be today what time
(that is to say, grace and circumstances
acting on your own good will)
will make of you tomorrow.
Only God could say what this new spirit
gradually forming within you will be.
Give Our Lord the benefit of believing that his hand is
      leading you,
and accept the anxiety of feeling yourself
in suspense and incomplete.

Hearts on Fire

Free Indeed!

Joseph A. Tetlow, SJ

You did a marvel, Lord Jesus Christ,
and make me feel beside myself in surprise.
My spirit glistens with Your rising.
I smile and smile with You,
I am drowning in the laughter of Your friends.
You have won, Lord, we know You have won!
You have defeated all the worst that we could do,
each alone and all together.
You crushed the power of darkness and of death
to walk peacefully again in our flesh,
now and forever.
Come to me, great Lord of Life,
as You come to all Your friends.
Send me to console those around me who hurt.
Come, and send Your friends into this daily world
to labor full of hope for the Reign of God.

Choosing Christ in the World

Index of Contributors

A

Arrupe, Pedro, 38, 46, 51, 151, 167
Aschenbrenner, George A., 43, 49, 130, 141

B

Barry, William A., 55, 75, 120, 142, 154
Byron, William, 152

C

Campbell, Paul Brian, 91, 106
Canisius, Peter, 57
Conroy, Maureen, 23, 48
Coutinho, Paul, 40, 45, 117, 138, 157
Creed, Bill, 128, 133

D

Delp, Alfred, 33
Doucet, Lyn Holley, 72, 115, 119
Dyckman, Katherine, 109, 132

E

English, John J., 32

F

Fagin, Gerald M., 37, 164
Fleming, David L., 13, 21, 26

W

List of Sources

[Page 3] William J. Young, trans., *Letters of St. Ignatius of Loyola* (Chicago: Loyola University Press, 1959), 240.

[Page 5] Adapted from Jim Manney, *A Simple, Life-Changing Prayer* (Chicago: Loyola Press, 2011), 1–2.

[Page 6] Ronald Modras, *Ignatian Humanism: A Dynamic Spirituality for the 21st Century* (Chicago: Loyola Press, 2004), 32.

[Page 8] Dennis Hamm, "Rummaging for God: Praying Backward through Your Day" (*America*, May 14, 1994). Used with the permission of the author.

[Page 9] Gerard Manley Hopkins, Robert Bridges, ed., *Poems of Gerard Manley Hopkins* (London: Humphrey Milford, 1918). Accessed via www.bartleby.com/122.

[Page 10] James Martin, *My Life with the Saints* (Chicago: Loyola Press, 2006), 81.

[Page 11] George W. Traub, *Ignatian Spirituality Reader: Contemporary Writings on St. Ignatius of Loyola, the Spiritual Exercises, Discernment, and More* (Chicago: Loyola Press, 2008), 255.

[Page 12] Vinita Hampton Wright, *Days of Deepening Friendship: For the Woman Who Wants Authentic Life with God* (Chicago: Loyola Press, 2009), 271.

[Page 13] David L. Fleming, *What Is Ignatian Spirituality?* (Chicago: Loyola Press, 2008), 52–53.

[Page 14] Ronald Modras, *Ignatian Humanism: A Dynamic Spirituality for the 21st Century* (Chicago: Loyola Press, 2004), 43.

[Page 15] William J. Young, trans., *Letters of St. Ignatius of Loyola* (Chicago: Loyola University Press, 1959), 240.

[Page 16] Jim Manney, "The Imaginary Boy", **ignatianspirituality.com/6656/the-imaginary-boy/** posted July 21, 2010.

[Page 17] Richard J. Hauser, *Finding God in Troubled Times* (Chicago: Loyola Press, 2002), 189–190.

[Page 21] David L. Fleming, *What Is Ignatian Spirituality?* (Chicago: Loyola Press, 2008), 57.

[Page 22] Margaret Silf, *Inner Compass: An Invitation to Ignatian Spirituality* (Chicago: Loyola Press, 1999), 211–212.

[Page 23] Maureen Conroy, *The Discerning Heart: Discovering a Personal God* (Chicago: Loyola Press, 1993), 15.

[Page 24] Chris Lowney, *Heroic Living: Discover Your Purpose and Change the World* (Chicago: Loyola Press, 2009), 27.

[Page 25] William J. O'Malley, *God: The Oldest Question* (Chicago: Loyola Press, 2000), 177–178.

[Page 26] David L. Fleming, *What Is Ignatian Spirituality?* (Chicago: Loyola Press, 2008), 58.

[Page 27] J. Michael Sparough, Jim Manney, and Tim Hipskind, *What's Your Decision? How to Make Choices with Confidence and Clarity* (Chicago: Loyola Press, 2010), 40.

[Page 28] Howard Gray, *As Leaven in the World: Catholic Perspectives on Faith, Vocation, and the Intellectual Life*, (Lanham, MD: Sheed and Ward, 2001), 322.

[Page 29] Vinita Hampton Wright, *Days of Deepening Friendship: For the Woman Who Wants Authentic Life with God* (Chicago: Loyola Press, 2009), 293.

[Page 30] Adapted from Gary Smith, *They Come Back Singing: Finding God with the Refugees* (Chicago: Loyola Press, 2008), 92–93.

[Page 31] Joseph A. Tetlow, *Making Choices in Christ: The Foundations of Ignatian Spirituality* (Chicago: Loyola Press, 2008), 82.

[Page 32] John J. English, *Spiritual Freedom: From an Experience of the Ignatian Exercises to the Art of Spiritual Guidance* (Chicago: Loyola Press, 1995), 133–134.

[Page 33] Mary Frances Coady, *With Bound Hands: A Jesuit in Nazi Germany: The Life and Selected Prison Letters of Alfred Delp* (Chicago: Loyola Press, 2003), 183.

[Page 37] Gerald M. Fagin, *Putting on the Heart of Christ: How the Spiritual Exercises Invite Us to a Virtuous Life* (Chicago: Loyola Press, 2010), 24–25.

[Page 38] Pedro Arrupe, as cited at **ignatianspirituality.com/ignatian-prayer/prayers-by-st -ignatius-and-others/fall-in-love**

[Page 39] Chris Lowney, *Heroic Living: Discover Your Purpose and Change the World* (Chicago: Loyola Press, 2009), 191–192.

[Page 40] Paul Coutinho, *How Big Is Your God? The Freedom to Experience the Divine* (Chicago: Loyola Press, 2007), 30.

[Page 41] Adapted from Margaret Silf, *Inner Compass: An Invitation to Ignatian Spirituality* (Chicago: Loyola Press, 1999), 23.

[Page 42] Jim Manney, **ignatianspirituality.com/7306/the -gratitude-list/** posted September 28, 2010.

[Page 43] George A. Aschenbrenner, *Stretched for Greater Glory: What to Expect from the Spiritual Exercises* (Chicago: Loyola Press, 2004), 38–39.

[Page 44] William J. Young, trans., *Letters of St. Ignatius of Loyola* (Chicago: Loyola University Press, 1959), 55.

[Page 45] Paul Coutinho, *How Big Is Your God? The Freedom to Experience the Divine* (Chicago: Loyola Press, 2007), 5–7.

[Page 46] Pedro Arrupe, *Other Apostolates Today: Selected Letters and Addresses III* (St. Louis: Institute of Jesuit Sources, 1981), 350.

[Page 47] Chris Lowney, *Heroic Leadership: Best Practices from a 450-Year-Old Company That Changed the World* (Chicago: Loyola Press, 2003), 251–252.

[Page 48] Maureen Conroy, *The Discerning Heart: Discovering a Personal God* (Chicago: Loyola Press, 1993), 71.

[Page 49] George A. Aschenbrenner, *Stretched for Greater Glory: What to Expect from the Spiritual Exercises* (Chicago: Loyola Press, 2004), 57.

[Page 50] Louis J. Puhl, trans., *The Spiritual Exercises of St. Ignatius* (Chicago: Loyola Press, 1968), section 316.

[Page 51] Pedro Arrupe, in final address at the General Congregation Thirty-Three, September 1983.

[Page 55] William A. Barry, *A Friendship Like No Other: Experiencing God's Amazing Embrace* (Chicago: Loyola Press, 2008), xiv–xv.

[Page 56] Margaret Silf, *Inner Compass: An Invitation to Ignatian Spirituality* (Chicago: Loyola Press, 1999), 25.

[Page 57] Michael Harter, ed. *Hearts on Fire: Praying with Jesuits* (Chicago: Loyola Press, 1993), 36.

[Page 58] Tim Muldoon, from **ignatianspirituality.com/ 6828/prayer-works/** posted August 10, 2010.

[Page 59] Kevin O'Brien, *The Ignatian Adventure: Experiencing the Spiritual Exercises of Saint Ignatius in Daily Life* (Chicago: Loyola Press, 2011), 53.

[Page 60] William J. Young, trans., *Letters of St. Ignatius of Loyola* (Chicago: Loyola University Press, 1959), 126–127.

[Page 61] Vinita Hampton Wright, *Days of Deepening Friendship: For the Woman Who Wants Authentic Life with God* (Chicago: Loyola Press, 2009), 174.

[Page 62] Joseph A. Tetlow, *Choosing Christ in the World* (St. Louis: The Institute of Jesuit Sources, 1989), 130. Used with permission.

[Page 63] Edward Peck, from **ignatianspirituality.com/ 4993/the-spirituality-of-cpr/** posted February 1, 2010.

[Page 64] John A. Veltri, *Orientations, Vol. 1* from **www.jesuits.ca/orientations/bob/page5.htm**

[Page 65] Gary Smith, *They Come Back Singing: Finding God with the Refugees* (Chicago: Loyola Press, 2008), 74–75.

[Page 70] Tim Muldoon, "Looking at the World as God's Project" adapted from **ignatianspirituality.com/7640/gods-project/** posted October 16, 2010.

[Page 71] William J. Young, trans., *Letters of St. Ignatius of Loyola* (Chicago: Loyola University Press, 1959), 441.

[Page 72] Lyn Holley Doucet, *A Healing Walk with St. Ignatius: Discovering God's Presence in Difficult Times* (Chicago: Loyola Press, 2002), 80–81.

[Page 73] William J. Young, trans., *Letters of St. Ignatius of Loyola* (Chicago: Loyola University Press, 1959), 134.

[Page 74] Gerard Manley Hopkins, *Poems and Prose* (1954) as cited in *The Saints' Guide to Happiness,* by Robert Ellsberg (New York: Image Books, 2005), 46.

[Page 75] Thomas M. Lucas, ed., *Spirit, Style, Story: Essays Honoring John W. Padberg, S.J.* (Chicago: Loyola Press, 2002), 43.

[Page 76] Jim Manney, "Washing Feet", adapted from **ignatianspirituality.com/5668/washing-feet/** posted April 15, 2010.

[Page 77] James Martin, *A Jesuit Off-Broadway: Behind the Scenes with Faith, Doubt, Forgiveness, and More* (Chicago: Loyola Press, 2007), 175.

[Page 78] William J. Young, trans., *Letters of St. Ignatius of Loyola* (Chicago: Loyola University Press, 1959), 405.

[Page 79] Chris Lowney, *Heroic Leadership: Best Practices from a 450-Year-Old Company That Changed the World* (Chicago: Loyola Press, 2003), 243–244.

[Page 80] Kevin O'Brien, *The Ignatian Adventure: Experiencing the Spiritual Exercises of Saint Ignatius in Daily Life* (Chicago: Loyola Press, 2011), 206.

[Page 83] Ronald Modras, *Ignatian Humanism: A Dynamic Spirituality for the 21st Century* (Chicago: Loyola Press, 2004), 46–47.

[Page 84] Vinita Hampton Wright, *Days of Deepening Friendship: For the Woman Who Wants Authentic Life with God* (Chicago: Loyola Press, 2009), 185–186.

[Page 85] Chris Lowney, *Heroic Living: Discover Your Purpose and Change the World* (Chicago: Loyola Press, 2009), 179.

[Page 86] Margaret Silf, *Inner Compass: An Invitation to Ignatian Spirituality* (Chicago: Loyola Press, 1999), 136.

[Page 87] Kevin O'Brien, *The Ignatian Adventure: Experiencing the Spiritual Exercises of Saint Ignatius in Daily Life* (Chicago: Loyola Press, 2011), 14–15 .

[Page 88] Maureen McCann Waldron, "God Doesn't Care How You Look" adapted from **ignatianspirituality.com/7016/a-startling-experiment/** posted August 31, 2010.

[Page 89] Tim Muldoon, ignatianspirituality.com/4886/ shared-silence posted January 16, 2010.

[Page 90] Joseph A. Tetlow, *Making Choices in Christ: The Foundations of Ignatian Spirituality* (Chicago: Loyola Press, 2008), 102–103.

[Page 92] Paul Brian Campbell, "Review of the Day for Managers", **ignatianspirituality.com/ignatian-prayer/the -examen/review-of-the-day-for-managers/** last accessed June 23, 2011.

[Page 93] Michael J. Daley and Lee P. Yeazell, eds., *In All Things: Everyday Prayers of Jesuit High School Students* (Chicago: Loyola Press, 2003), 120.

[Page 94] Chris Lowney, *Heroic Living: Discover Your Purpose and Change the World* (Chicago: Loyola Press, 2009), 152–153.

[Page 95] Margaret Silf, *Inner Compass: An Invitation to Ignatian Spirituality* (Chicago: Loyola Press, 1999), 59.

[Page 99] Ronald Modras, *Ignatian Humanism: A Dynamic Spirituality for the 21st Century* (Chicago: Loyola Press, 2004), 2.

[Page 100] Jim Manney, adapted from **ignatianspirituality.com/3040/what-i-like-about-ignatius -loyola/** posted July 31, 2009.

[Page 101] Louis J. Puhl, trans., *The Spiritual Exercises of St. Ignatius* (Chicago: Loyola Press, 1968).

[Page 102] Documents of the 34th General Congregation of the Society of Jesus; Decree 26, no. 8.

[Page 103] Louis J. Puhl, trans., *The Spiritual Exercises of St. Ignatius* (Chicago: Loyola Press, 1968) section 235.

[Page 103] Michael Harter, ed., *Hearts on Fire: Praying with Jesuits* (Chicago: Loyola Press, 1993), 58.

[Page 104] Amy Welborn, *The Words We Pray: Discovering the Richness of Traditional Catholic Prayers* (Chicago: Loyola Press, 2005), 140–141.

[Page 105] Jim Manney, "What's Next?" from **ignatianspirituality.com/6072/whats-next/** posted May 27, 2010.

[Page 107] Paul Brian Campbell, unpublished papers, Loyola Press.

[Page 108] Tim Muldoon, adapted from **ignatianspirituality.com/8245/formation/** posted December 3, 2010.

[Page 109] Katherine Dyckman, Mary Garvin, and Elizabeth Liebert, *The Spiritual Exercises Reclaimed: Uncovering Liberating Possibilities for Women* (New York: Paulist Press, 2001), 31–32.

[Page 110] Jules J. Toner, *Discerning God's Will: Ignatius's Teaching on Christian Decision Making* (St. Louis: Institute of Jesuit Sources, 1991), 13.

[Page 113] David L. Fleming, *Draw Me into Your Friendship: The Spiritual Exercises* (St. Louis: The Institute of Jesuit Sources, 1996), 23.

[Page 114] Joseph A. Tetlow, "Examen: Persons in Relationship," *Review for Religious* 61 (Mar/Apr 2002), 118.

[Page 115] Lyn Holley Doucet, *A Healing Walk with St. Ignatius: Discovering God's Presence in Difficult Times* (Chicago: Loyola Press, 2002), 12.

[Page 116] William J. Young, trans., *Letters of St. Ignatius of Loyola* (Chicago: Loyola University Press, 1959), 51–52.

[Page 117] Paul Coutinho, *How Big Is Your God? The Freedom to Experience the Divine* (Chicago: Loyola Press, 2007), 138.

[Page 118] William J. Young, trans., *Letters of St. Ignatius of Loyola* (Chicago: Loyola University Press, 1959), 363.

[Page 119] Lyn Holley Doucet, *A Healing Walk with St. Ignatius: Discovering God's Presence in Difficult Times* (Chicago: Loyola Press, 2002), 119–120.

[Page 120] William A. Barry, *Letting God Come Close: An Approach to the Ignatian Spiritual Exercises* (Chicago: Loyola Press, 2001), 55.

[Page 121] Margaret Silf, *Inner Compass: An Invitation to Ignatian Spirituality* (Chicago: Loyola Press, 1999), 209.

[Page 122] Gerard Manley Hopkins, Robert Bridges, ed., *Poems of Gerard Manley Hopkins* (London: Humphrey Milford, 1918). Accessed via **www.bartleby.com/122**.

[Page 123] William J. Young, trans., *Letters of St. Ignatius of Loyola* (Chicago: Loyola University Press, 1959), 11.

[Page 124] James Martin, *A Jesuit Off-Broadway: Behind the Scenes with Faith, Doubt, Forgiveness, and More* (Chicago: Loyola Press, 2007), 214.

[Page 127] Joseph A. Tetlow, *Choosing Christ in the World* (St. Louis: The Institute of Jesuit Sources), 128.

[Page 129] Bill Creed, unpublished papers. Used with permission.

[Page 130] George A. Aschenbrenner, *Stretched for Greater Glory: What to Expect from the Spiritual Exercises* (Chicago: Loyola Press, 2004), 6.

[Page 131] Louis J. Puhl, trans., *The Spiritual Exercises of St. Ignatius* (Chicago: Loyola Press, 1968), 2.

[Page 132] Katherine Dyckman, Mary Garvin, and Elizabeth Liebert, *The Spiritual Exercises Reclaimed: Uncovering Liberating Possibilities for Women* (New York: Paulist Press, 2001), 7.

[Page 133] Bill Creed, unpublished papers. Used with permission.

[Page 134] Louis J. Puhl, trans., *The Spiritual Exercises of St. Ignatius* (Chicago: Loyola Press, 1968), section 326.

[Page 135] Joseph A. Tetlow, *Making Choices in Christ: The Foundations of Ignatian Spirituality* (Chicago: Loyola Press, 2008), 108–109.

[Page 136] Mark E. Thibodeaux, *God's Voice Within: The Ignatian Way to Discover God's Will* (Chicago: Loyola Press, 2010), 82.

[Page 137] Ronald Modras, *Ignatian Humanism: A Dynamic Spirituality for the 21st Century* (Chicago: Loyola Press, 2004), 23.

[Page 138] Paul Coutinho, *How Big Is Your God? The Freedom to Experience the Divine* (Chicago: Loyola Press, 2007), 70.

[Page 141] George A. Aschenbrenner, *Stretched for Greater Glory: What to Expect from the Spiritual Exercises* (Chicago: Loyola Press, 2004), 8.

[Page 142] William A. Barry, *Letting God Come Close: An Approach to the Ignatian Spiritual Exercises* (Chicago: Loyola Press, 2001), 34–36.

[Page 143] J. Michael Sparough, Jim Manney, Tim Hipskind, *What's Your Decision? How to Make Choices with Confidence and Clarity* (Chicago: Loyola Press, 2010), 98–99.

[Page 144] Mark E. Thibodeaux, *God's Voice Within: The Ignatian Way to Discover God's Will* (Chicago: Loyola Press, 2010), 57–58.

[Page 145] J. Michael Sparough, Jim Manney, Tim Hipskind, *What's Your Decision? How to Make Choices with Confidence and Clarity* (Chicago: Loyola Press, 2010), 27.

[Page 146] J. Michael Sparough, Jim Manney, Tim Hipskind, *What's Your Decision? How to Make Choices with Confidence and Clarity* (Chicago: Loyola Press, 2010), 51–52.

[Page 147] William J. Young, trans., *St. Ignatius' Own Story: As Told to Luis Gonzalez de Camara* (Chicago: Loyola University Press, 1998), 10.

[Page 149] Adapted from Mark E. Thibodeaux, *God's Voice Within: The Ignatian Way to Discover God's Will* (Chicago: Loyola Press, 2010), 34–35.

[Page 150] Documents of the 34th General Congregation of the Society of Jesus; Decree 26, no. 6.

[Page 151] Michael Harter, ed., *Hearts on Fire: Praying with Jesuits* (Chicago: Loyola Press, 2004), 97.

[Page 153] Adapted from William Byron, *Jesuit Saturdays: Sharing the Ignatian Spirit with Friends and Colleagues* (Chicago: Loyola Press, 2000), 70–71.

[Page 154] Thomas M. Lucas, ed., *Spirit, Style, Story: Essays Honoring John W. Padberg* (Chicago: Loyola Press, 2002), 40.

[Page 157] Paul Coutinho, *How Big Is Your God? The Freedom to Experience the Divine* (Chicago: Loyola Press, 2003), 77–78.

[Page 158] Vinita Hampton Wright, *Days of Deepening Friendship: For the Woman Who Wants Authentic Life with God* (Chicago: Loyola Press, 2009), 123.

[Page 159] James Martin, *My Life with the Saints* (Chicago: Loyola Press, 2006), 85.

[Page 161] Chris Lowney, *Heroic Leadership: Best Practices from a 450-Year-Old Company That Changed the World* (Chicago: Loyola Press, 2003), 119–120.

[Page 162] Mark E. Thibodeaux, *God's Voice Within: The Ignatian Way to Discover God's Will* (Chicago: Loyola Press, 2010), 147.

[Page 163] Michael J. Daley and Lee P. Yeazell, eds. *In All Things: Everyday Prayers of Jesuit High School Students* (Chicago: Loyola Press, 2003), 121.

[Page 164] Gerald M. Fagin, *Putting on the Heart of Christ: How the Spiritual Exercises Invite Us to a Virtuous Life* (Chicago: Loyola Press, 2010), 50.

[Page 165] William O'Malley, *God: The Oldest Question* (Chicago: Loyola Press, 2000), 194.

[Page 166] Adapted from William J. Young, trans., *Letters of St. Ignatius of Loyola* (Chicago: Loyola University Press, 1959), 20.

[Page 167] Pedro Arrupe, *The Spiritual Legacy of Pedro Arrupe, S.J.* (New York Province of the Society of Jesus, 1985).

[Page 168] Pierre Teilhard de Chardin, Michael Harter, ed., *Hearts on Fire: Praying with Jesuits* (Chicago: Loyola Press, 2004), 102.

[Page 169] Joseph A. Tetlow, *Choosing Christ in the World* (St. Louis: The Institute of Jesuit Sources, 1989), 105.

7